Pagan Portals
&
Shaman Pathways

...an ever-growing library of shared knowledge.

Moon Books has created two unique series where leading authors
and practitioners come together to share their knowledge,
passion and expertise across the complete Pagan spectrum. If you
would like to contribute to either series, our proposal procedure
is simple and quick, just visit our website (www.MoonBooks.net)
and click on Author Inquiry to begin the process.

If you are a reader with a comment about a book or a suggestion
for a title we'd love to hear from you! You can find us at
facebook.com/MoonBooks or you can keep up to date with new
releases etc on our dedicated Portals page at facebook.com/
paganportalsandshamanpathways/

'Moon Books has achieved that rare feat of being synonymous
with top-quality authorship AND being endlessly innovative and
exciting.'
Kate Large, Pagan Dawn

T0149051

Pagan Portals

Animal Magic, Rachel Patterson
An introduction to the world of animal magic and working with animal spirit guides

Australian Druidry, Julie Brett
Connect with the magic of the southern land, its seasons, animals, plants and spirits

Blacksmith Gods, Pete Jennings
Exploring dark folk tales and customs alongside the magic and myths of the blacksmith Gods through time and place

Brigid, Morgan Daimler
Meeting the Celtic Goddess of Poetry, Forge, and Healing Well

By Spellbook & Candle, Mélusine Draco
Why go to the bother of cursing, when a bottling or binding can be just as effective?

By Wolfsbane & Mandrake Root, Mélusine Draco
A study of poisonous plants, many of which have beneficial uses in both domestic medicine and magic

Candle Magic, Lucya Starza
Using candles in simple spells, seasonal rituals and essential craft techniques

Celtic Witchcraft, Mabh Savage
Wield winds of wyrd, dive into pools of wisdom; walk side by side with the Tuatha Dé Danann

Dancing with Nemetona, Joanna van der Hoeven
An in-depth look at a little-known Goddess who can help bring peace and sanctuary into your life

Fairy Witchcraft, Morgan Daimler
A guidebook for those seeking a path that combines modern Neopagan witchcraft with the older Celtic Fairy Faith

God-Speaking, Judith O'Grady
What can we do to save the planet? Three Rs are not enough. Reduce, reuse, recycle...and religion

Gods and Goddesses of Ireland,
Meet the Gods and Goddesses of Pagan Ireland in myth and modern practice

Grimalkyn: The Witch's Cat, Martha Gray
A mystical insight into the cat as a power animal

Hedge Riding, Harmonia Saille
The hedge is the symbolic boundary between the two worlds and this book will teach you how to cross that hedge

Hedge Witchcraft, Harmonia Saille
Learning by experiencing is about trusting your instincts and connecting with your inner spirit

Hekate, Vivienne Moss
The Goddess of Witches, Queen of Shades and Shadows, and the ever-eternal Dark Muse haunts the pages of this poetic devotional, enchanting those who love Her with the charm only this Dark Goddess can bring

Runes, Kylie Holmes

The Runes are a set of 24 symbols that are steeped in history, myths and legends. This book offers practical and accessible information for anyone to understand this ancient form of divination

Sacred Sex and Magick, Web PATH Center

Wrap up ecstasy in love to create powerful magick, spells and healing

Spirituality without Structure, Nimue Brown

The only meaningful spiritual journey is the one you consciously undertake

The Awen Alone, Joanna van der Hoeven

An introductory guide for the solitary Druid

The Cailleach, Rachel Patterson

Goddess of the ancestors, wisdom that comes with age, the weather, time, shape-shifting and winter

The Morrigan, Morgan Daimler

On shadowed wings and in raven's call, meet the ancient Irish Goddess of war, battle, prophecy, death, sovereignty, and magic

Urban Ovate, Brendan Howlin

Simple, accessible techniques to bring Druidry to the wider public

Your Faery Magic, Halo Quin

Tap into your Natural Magic and become the Fey you are

Zen Druidry, Joanna van der Hoeven
Zen teachings and Druidry combine to create a peaceful life path
that is completely dedicated to the here and now

Shaman Pathways

Aubry's Dog, Melusine Draco
A practical and essential guide to using canine magical energies

Black Horse White Horse, Mélusine Draco
Feel the power and freedom as Black Horse, White Horse guides
you down the magical path of this most noble animal

Celtic Chakras, Elen Sentier
Tread the British native shaman's path, explore the Goddess
hidden in the ancient stories; walk the Celtic chakra spiral
labyrinth

Druid Shaman, Danu Forest
A practical guide to Celtic shamanism with exercises and
techniques as well as traditional lore for exploring the Celtic
Otherworld

Elen of the Ways, Elen Sentier
British shamanism has largely been forgotten: the reindeer
Goddess of the ancient Boreal forest is shrouded in mystery...
follow her deer-trods to rediscover her old ways

Following the Deer Trods, Elen Sentier
A practical handbook for anyone wanting to begin the old British
paths. Follows on from Elen of the Ways

Trees of the Goddess, Elen Sentier
Work with the trees of the Goddess and the old ways of Britain

Way of the Faery Shaman, Flavia Kate Peters
Your practical insight into Faeries and the elements they engage
to unlock real magic that is waiting to help you

Web of Life, Yvonne Ryves
A new approach to using ancient ways in these contemporary
and often challenging times to weave your life path

What people are saying about

Pagan Portals: Rhiannon Divine Queen of the Celtic Britons

Sophisticated and elegant, steeped in scholarship and passionately written, Telyndru's offering to Rhiannon will take you on a journey deep into the heart of mystery, sovereignty and connection. Within these pages you will discover the tools necessary to develop a lasting and meaningful relationship with Rhiannon. To connect to the Divine Queen we must ask her to stop and notice us, Telyndru offers you a guiding hand to understand this process and move into relationship with the Goddess. What you hold in your hands is priceless, for this is a gift of inspiration. **Kristoffer Hughes**, author of *From the Cauldron Born: Exploring the Magic of Welsh Legend and Lore* and *Head of the Anglesey Druid Order*

Rhiannon: Divine Queen of the Celtic Britons is the perfect introduction to a Welsh Goddess who can be elusive and ephemeral as well as profound and present. In this slim introduction Jhenah Telyndru has combined solid academic information, myth, spiritual devotion and practical suggestions that anyone could incorporate into their own lives. The end result is a book that invites the reader to delve deep into the history of Welsh mythology and create a profound connection to this powerful Goddess. A must read for anyone interested in either Rhiannon or Welsh deities more generally.
Morgan Daimler, best-selling author of *The Morrigan* and *Fairies: A Guide to the Celtic Fair Folk*

Jhenah Telyndru's *Rhiannon: Divine Queen of the Celtic Britons* is a real treasure-trove of lore and wisdom regarding this beloved

Welsh goddess. The first half of this book gives us a brilliant scholarly introduction to Her, while the second half offers insights into developing an immediate and first-hand relationship with this Sovereign deity. By combining the academic with the experiential this work really stands out in today's modern goddess literature. Another superb offering by Jhenah Telyndru.

Joanna van der Hoeven, best-selling author of *The Awen Alone: Walking the Path of the Solitary Druid* and *The Crane Bag: A Druid's Guide to Ritual Tools and Practices*, Druid Priestess and Director of Druid College UK

As both literary character and goddess, Rhiannon is hard to get to know. But Jhenah Telyndru's book brings her to life. Here you find the historical and literary sources studied with logical clarity and precision, as well as a gentle and loving present-day devotional interpretation. This book is not only an informative text: it is also a work of art.

Brendan Myers, Ph.D., author of *Reclaiming Civilization: A Case for Optimism for the Future of Humanity* and *The Earth, The Gods and The Soul - A History of Pagan Philosophy*

With a clear voice for storytelling and a deft hand at complex and multidisciplinary research, Jhenah Telyndru's love and devotion to her goddess shines through with every page. This book is satisfyingly academic while being deeply moving and practical for anyone looking to build or deepen into a relationship with this goddess. I highly recommend this book for new seekers and experienced practitioners alike.

River Devora, priest and founder of the Strong Roots and Wide Branches Polytheist Learning Community

A new entry in Moon Books' excellent Pagan Portals series, Jhenah Telyndru's *Rhiannon: Divine Queen of the Celtic Britons* presents us with an introduction to this enigmatic Goddess that is both lyrical and academic. Ms. Telyndru is well equipped to take on this challenge. The founder and leader of the Sisterhood of Avalon, with a Master's in Celtic Studies from the University of Wales Trinity Saint David, she is steeped in medieval Celtic literature, ancient archaeology, and Welsh culture – all of which enable her to read early sources with special clarity, and then relate those sources to the modern spiritual and cultural concerns of her readers. At once practical and poetic, mystical and scholarly, Jhenah Telyndru's *Rhiannon: Divine Queen of the Celtic Britons* teaches us much about a popular yet ill-understood deity, who we think we know, but don't really. In consequence, I recommend it highly.

Segomâros Widugeni, formerly Aedh Rua, author of *Celtic Flame*

So much more than brilliant, precise scholarship, *Rhiannon: Divine Queen of the Celtic Britons* is an exquisite melding of history, mythology and lore. Jhenah Telyndru entices a depth of historical insight out of rich range of resources to place it at your doorstep in an engaging, evocative manner and she takes dynamic relationship with Rhiannon out of ritual confines to place it actively in the nuances of everyday life. This important work is a linguistic archeological treasure; an invitation to hone awareness of how we know what we know; and an inspired guide for spiritual practice. Jhenah follows the trail of historical breadcrumbs to give us a feast, complete with ancient tales, poetry and song. Every morsel is a delight to savour.

Tiffany Lazic, author of *The Great Work: Self-Knowledge and Healing Through the Wheel of the Year*

Rhiannon: Divine Queen of the Celtic Britons is an excellent introduction to Rhiannon and Her world. Jhenah's warm, engaging style illuminates a mysterious Lady like a medieval manuscript, weaving history and mythology together like the worlds Rhiannon traverses: effortlessly and with grace. A well-researched and powerful aid to those who seek to know Her, at any level of engagement.

Rev. Tamara L. Siuda, Founder of the House of Netjer, author of *The Ancient Egyptian Daybook* and *The Ancient Egyptian Prayerbook*

Pagan Portals

Rhiannon
Divine Queen of the Celtic Britons

Pagan Portals

Rhiannon

Divine Queen of the Celtic Britons

Jhenah Telyndru

Winchester, UK
Washington, USA

First published by Moon Books, 2018
Moon Books is an imprint of John Hunt Publishing Ltd., Laurel House, Station Approach,
Alresford, Hants, SO24 9JH, UK
office1@jhpbooks.net
www.johnhuntpublishing.com
www.moon-books.net

For distributor details and how to order please visit the 'Ordering' section on our website.

Text copyright: Jhenah Telyndru 2017

ISBN: 978 1 78535 468 7
978 1 78535 469 4 (ebook)
Library of Congress Control Number: 2017940004

A CIP catalogue record for this book is available from the British Library.

Design: Stuart Davies

Printed and bound by CPI Group (UK) Ltd, Croydon, CR0 4YY, UK

We operate a distinctive and ethical publishing philosophy in
all areas of our business, from our global network of authors to
production and worldwide distribution.

Contents

To the Mothers.

Acknowledgements

Nothing is created in a vacuum, and to enumerate everything and everyone that made up the matrix of support that assisted in the birth of this book will be impossible, so I will do my best to hit the highlights.

First and foremost, I would like to thank Trevor Greenfield for the trust he placed in me when he approached me to write this volume for Moon Books. His patience, guidance, and support, as well as those of the whole Moon Books team, are deeply appreciated.

I am incredibly grateful for the Gaulish expertise and open sharing of River Devora, whose devotion to the Matronae is inspirational. My gratitude for the generosity of Morgan Daimler similarly knows no bounds; her ability (and cheerful willingness) to point me towards the correct Irish resources, including those she herself has translated, has been of enormous assistance.

There are so many reasons for me to feel deeply blessed and appreciative for the presence in my life of my dear Sister and friend Lori Feldmann; in this case, I am grateful for her editing magic and for all of her support and feedback.

I am so very thankful for the Sisterhood of Avalon, for all of my beautiful Sisters, and to all who have shared sacred space with me—especially those times, under the Full Moon, when we call to the Divine Queen...

I am grateful to my family, both of blood and of choice. Thank you for your support, for your understanding, and for always gifting me with a soft place to land. Thank you especially to my children for being so understanding of my sometimes-crazy process. I love you both so!

And finally, I want to thank my beloved James for always believing in me... for holding up a mirror of truth, and showing me what I need most to see. Thank you for helping me to remember. Thank you, too, for helping me to forget.

Introduction

Climbing the Mound

Winding our way up the yew-lined pathway which led us deeper and deeper into a shadowland of overhanging trees standing in stark contrast to the ruins of Castle Narberth, whose stones were bare and hot in the summer sun, it was easy to feel as if we were passing into another world. That the long, uphill path required that we pass over a small bridge and under the spreading branches of an enormous hawthorn tree only reinforced the feeling that the borders of the Otherworld were close at hand. We stopped there and circled beneath the holy thorn, centering and chanting and pouring out a libation as an offering to the spirits of place, before we continued on to emerge from the shadow of trees and stand before the gentle rise of the rounded hill. Surrounded by a bramble hedge, the hill's green mantle was drenched in slanting sunlight beneath the bright blue sky.

A moment of silence. A breath. A heart-felt prayer before we continued forward. Step by intentional step, we made our way up to the crest of the hill, and saw the whole of the landscape spread out before us... an almost timeless patchwork of farmlands, the steeples of churches, and the peaks of centuries-old buildings. There, a copse of trees... here, the stone ruins of the Norman castle we had just visited... always, the white embellishments of sheep grazing serenely against the verdant quilt of the countryside. It was a beautiful sight, but we were there with hopes of seeing something more. A wonder, perhaps, or a vision of what was. A glimpse of the Lady of this land, whom legend says emerged from this very mound, or perhaps one like it, in pursuit of that which she desired.

Where before we had circled beneath the tree, joined in chant and in intention, now this group of 20-odd women instead fanned out, organically seeking a place of their own on the hillside. Some sat, others stood. Still others chose to stay in motion, tracing the diameter of the hill. All maintained a space of sacred silence, keenly aware of the mythic import of the moment. For tradition teaches that the Gorsedd Arberth, the legendary mound that some identify with this very hill, was a place of magic... and those who came to stand upon this hill—especially a king... or in our case, a group of women actively seeking our personal sovereignty—would either experience a great wonder, or be subject to terrible blows. We all hoped for the former, but knew that even the latter—albeit in a more metaphorical sense—would have something to teach us about who we were and our work in the world.

There is something powerful about embodying myth, something transformational about seeking Source out in the world in order to discover that the sacred landscape exists both around and within us as we reflect those energies back upon ourselves. Joseph Campbell wrote, "myths are public dreams, dreams are private myths." Myths are the dreams of a culture, representing the needs and perspectives of a people in the same way our personal dreams help us to process and understand our own desires, the ways in which we see ourselves and, consequently, our place in the universe. To consciously come into alignment with legends and folktales is to see ourselves in more cosmological terms. We take ourselves outside of time when we move ourselves into a liminal space where all possibilities coexist, and where the truth of who and what we are is not limited to that which we are able to imagine. And so, a mythic tale of an Otherworldly woman who emerges from a magical hill astride a white horse can become our own story, its embedded symbols become vessels that we can fill with our most secret selves, and the twists and turns of the plot reflect the map of our own unfolding lives.

To understand Rhiannon, we too must undertake a journey

into unknown lands to pursue that which we most desire. We must excavate the layers of her myth, decode the meaning of her symbols, and seek to restore the significance of her very name. We cannot pursue her directly, for the seemingly slow and steady gait of her magnificent white mount ever outpaces even the swiftest of steeds. Yet, if we but call to her and ask for what we need, she immediately stops and answers us, a generous and gracious Lady whose bag of plenty can fill us, and whose birds can soothe our deepest hurts and call us back to the lands of the living once more. And so, as we embark upon this reflection on Rhiannon, the Divine Queen of the Celtic Britons, let us call to her and speak our need with all of our hearts:

Lady Rhiannon, Holy Sovereign
Great Queen of the Otherworld:

Teach us the way of the White Horse -
That we may journey on the paths of this world
With clarity of purpose and strength of heart,
Holding fast to the Sacred Center of our inner truth
Even in the face of all hardships and injustices.

Teach us the way of the Three Birds -
That we may find courage in times of darkness
And relief from our burdens and cares.
That the parts of ourselves we have thought long dead
May arise in joy and gladness once more.

Teach us the way of the Divine Mother -
That we may nurture truth, birth understanding,
And act with endless compassion for ourselves and others.
Show us the ways of unconditional love and loyalty
That we may know when to hold tight… and when we must
    let go.

3

Teach us the way of the Great Queen -
That we may walk in this world in our power,
In unflinching pursuit of our true purpose,
And unafraid to ask for that which we need
As we come fully into the light of our Sovereignty.

Lady Rhiannon, Holy Sovereign
Great Queen of the Otherworld:

Teach us to be free.

Chapter One

The Tapestry of Time

To write about Rhiannon is to undertake a journey. While she has a mythology around her, her origins are obscure. While she has many modern-day devotees, she is never identified as a Goddess in any of the primary source material. While she appears to have ancient Pagan attributes, her tales were written during the medieval period in a Christianized country that did not even exist politically when the Island of Britain was Pagan. There are no known ancient prayers or rituals in her honor. We have no known cult centers or devotional altars dedicated to Rhiannon. We have only a breadcrumb trail of clues to follow which are made up of syncretic resonances, embedded symbolism, and a mythic heritage which begs to be traced back through the Otherworldly veils of history. How then do we approach this revered Lady? How can we best know her as Goddess?

Neo-Pagans generally have come to expect to interact with divinities either from within a newly-created tradition that recasts them to work in a neoteric system like Wicca, for example, or else seeks to reconstruct the old ways with as much cultural authenticity as possible. The latter is possible because many ancient societies have left behind a rich corpus of written work detailing the stories, rituals, and observances to honor their Gods. Unfortunately, the Celts did not do the same, preferring to transmit their sacred stories through oral tradition rather than setting them down into writing. Caesar writes of this phenomenon in his *Gallic War*:

> They [the Druids] are said there to learn by heart a great number of verses; accordingly some remain in the course of training twenty years. Nor do they regard it lawful to

commit these to writing, though in almost all other matters, in their public and private transactions, they use Greek characters. That practice they seem to me to have adopted for two reasons; because they neither desire their doctrines to be divulged among the mass of the people, nor those who learn, to devote themselves the less to the efforts of memory, relying on writing; since it generally occurs to most men, that, in their dependence on writing, they relax their diligence in learning thoroughly, and their employment of the memory. (Caesar, *Gallic War*, Chapter 14)

Regardless of the intention, the result of this practice is that unlike many other ancient cultures, the beliefs, religious practices, and myths of the Pagan Celts were not written down until relatively late, especially in areas that had been annexed by the Roman Empire, such as Gaul and Britain. It is important to note that Druidism — the priestly caste which performed the ceremonies and sacrifices, served as judges and mediators, acted as augurs and healers, and transmitted the lore as bards and poets — was outlawed in Gaul in the first century CE and finally wiped out in Britain during the siege of the Island of Anglesey by Roman troops in 61 CE. The primary keepers of religious knowledge in these areas, therefore, were mostly eradicated, and so it is posited that what may have remained did so as folk memory and practice which were passed down from generation to generation through oral tradition.

As time progressed, Britain, like almost all of Europe, became Christianized and endured wave after wave of invasion, first from Germanic tribes after Rome withdrew and then from the Normans. Eventually, several nations arose on the island: Wales, made up of a network of kingdoms to the west of Offa's Dyke, most retained the culture of the Celtic Britons, and resonated strongly with the other Brythonic people of Cornwall and Brittany; Scotland, which was more closely aligned culturally with the Irish and Manx; and England, which was primarily influenced by Germanic and Norman cultures, rather than those of the Celts.

When whatever myths and legends which had endured in oral tradition since Celtic Pagan times finally began to be redacted in the Welsh medieval period, we can assume that the tales had evolved over time, and, as written, we can see that they are greatly influenced by the laws and social mores of the contemporary medieval audience. The stories which comprise The Four Branches of the mythic cycle we know as *Y Mabinogi* were written down sometime between the 11th and 13th centuries, possibly by clerics, or otherwise by lay scholars interested in preserving Welsh culture at a time when Wales had lost its independence to Anglo-Norman England. Ostensibly, because of this desire to archive and preserve these tales, it is unlikely that the redactors themselves made any substantive changes to the stories as they had received them, and indeed, there are phrases included in the narratives which were typical of the mnemonic and onomastic devices known to have been used during oral recitation (Davies, 1993). If these tales have their roots in Pagan Celtic tradition, therefore, any shifts of characterization or symbolism are likely a natural result of evolution of the tales over time, and not reflective of any kind of political or religious agenda.

The characters we generally assume to be divinities are never identified as such in any existent tales; they are, however, often depicted as supernatural or larger-than-life figures. These stories feature a comfortability with magic and the Otherworld which may seem unusual to us when we consider that Wales was a wholly Christian country at the time they were committed to writing; the Four Branches are filled with faery queens, magicians, shape changers, giants, visits to the Otherworld, magical animals, and even the creation of a woman out of flowers. Textual references are made to religious traditions performed "in the custom of the time", which seem to refer to Pagan rites and rituals from the pre-Christian era. Where scholars of *Y Mabinogi* and contemporary tales embrace the theory that these stories have Pagan roots, they are careful to say that there is no direct proof of this connection, noting, for example, that the similarity of character names with divine figures in other Celtic mythos (such as Rhiannon's second husband, Manawydan fab Llŷr and the Irish God of the sea Manannán mac Lir) and the appearance of common international folk motifs (for example, the king obtains sovereignty by sleeping with a representative of the land) could instead be the result of cultural exchanges in the early medieval period; everyone likes to tell a good story, and these tales may well have been influenced by stories originating in Ireland or on the continent (Jackson, 1961).

There is a similar problem with concluding that British folk customs, such as the winter mumming tradition of the Mari Lwyd (Grey Mare) or those of the Hunting of the Wren, are remnants of Celtic Pagan practices that survived through time. While the symbol sets included in these traditions—a veiled horse's skull with a working jaw used as a pantomime in a ritualized exchange between mummers and individual households in turn, and the capture, displaying, and parading of a tiny, otherwise-protected bird from house to house in order to confer luck and fertility—appear to be very Pagan in origin, they may simply reflect the unconscious needs of an agrarian people who worked the same land, with essentially the same technology, and faced the same survival challenges during the winter months as their ancient ancestors. Since these practices can only be attested to from the 17th century forward, there is again no direct proof of their ancient Pagan origins—but this need not diminish the power of these practices, both psychologically and practically (Wood, 1997).

It is important to again stress that there are no known temples, altar inscriptions, or votive offerings dedicated to Rhiannon; the archaeological record simply does not directly support the idea of her divinity, nor that of any character in existent Welsh lore. However, if we consider the ways in which cultures change and grow over time, especially as new influences and challenges arise, it is possible that a similar process occurs when it comes to the form and even the name of a culture's gods. It is fairly well attested that in the process of becoming Christianized, the gods of a people often became local saints, not necessarily canonical as far as the Church of Rome was concerned, but honored and appealed to as intercessors nonetheless; oftentimes, these saints retained attributes or areas of influence from their godly past. Perhaps the most famous example of this is the transition of the Irish Goddess Brigid to the beloved St. Brigid; both shared a cult site in Cill Dara/Kildare, both were associated with the forge, healing, and creativity, and both had an eternal flame burning in their honor—a devotion that was extinguished during the Reformation, and rekindled in Kildare once more in 1993.

If we accept that this has happened during the transition from Paganism to Christianity, certainly then there have to have been other times when the Gods evolved and changed forms. In Western European traditions, we speak of a reconstructed Indo-European "mother culture" which is believed to have been the origin point for certain language groups and their attendant cultures. The Celtic language family is a branch off of this Proto-Indo-European language tree, and it is possible to trace the approximate times and places where new languages—and, ostensibly, their associated cultural forms—broke off from the main branch. As the Celtic peoples and their ideas began to spread across Europe from what is believed to be their origin points in the upper Danube valley in the 13th century BCE, their tribal nature saw distinct cultural groups develop depending on where they settled (Cunliffe,1997).These differentiations likely arose from a combination of integrating with the peoples who already inhabited these lands, the adoption of Celtic cultural ideas by other peoples, and as a result of the challenges presented by the lands themselves.

Although Celtic territories once spanned from as far east as Turkey, as far west as the Iberian peninsula, and as far north as the British Isles and Ireland at their greatest extent, the two major subgroups branching off of the Common Celtic language was Continental Celtic and Insular Celtic (Koch, 2006). These groups formed their own branches and according to one linguistic model, from Continental Celtic arose Celtiberian, Gaulish, Galatian, Leptonic, and Noric—all of which are extinct. Insular Celtic branched into two major groups: Brythonic (P-Celtic), from which came Welsh, Cornish, and Breton; and Goidelic (Q-Celtic), out of which evolved Irish, Manx, and Scots Gaelic—each of which had their own stages of development (Sifter, 2008). The modern iterations of these languages survive at various levels of success, despite long-term attempts by the English to suppress and extinguish them.

While this may seem like a strange side-track to a conversation about Rhiannon, it is a critical piece for understanding several key ideas. First, it underscores the reality that the Celts were not a monolithic culture; there were Celtic peoples whose languages had evolved so distinctively that although they were related linguistically, the speakers would not have been able to understand each other. Second, it is important to realize that not only were the Celtic peoples separated from each other in space, but also in time. Their cultures existed in various stages during the Pagan period for at least 1000 years, and their different historical experiences had great impact on the further development of their cultures (Cunliffe, 1997). For example, the Roman conquest of Gaul and Britain changed the trajectories of these peoples and their religious forms in a way that we do not see in Ireland, a critical distinction when attempting to study the mythos of any of these cultures. Lastly, it is important to realize that *Y Mabinogi* and contemporary tales were written down in Middle Welsh, a language which did not exist until the 12th century, and that the nation known as Wales didn't even come into being until the 6th century CE, which was approximately the same time that all of Britain had been Christianized (Sifter, 2008).

So, while it is true that Rhiannon is not identified as a Goddess in *Y Mabinogi*, nor have we found any artifactual proof of her worship, or any observation of her cultus by contemporary ancient writers, perhaps the conclusion that this is because she and other legendary Welsh figures are not divinities is incorrect. Perhaps we have found no shrines, images, or inscriptions dedicated to Rhiannon because there simply could not have been any as a consequence of the pre-Roman Celtic preference to worship in sacred groves and not to write sacred things down. Indeed, the very language of Rhiannon's name had not developed until long after the Pagan Celtic period in Britain had ended. Perhaps then, in order to explore the truth of Rhiannon's potentially divine nature, we must follow a more subtle route - one which requires a deep reading of her mythos, an examination of linguistic evidence, the identification of medieval elements in her tale to discern the provenance of what remains, and a comparative study of similar Goddesses both from adjacent and precursor cultures. What follows is an exploration of this very path, undertaken in hopes of gaining a deeper understanding of Rhiannon.

Chapter Two

Primary Sources

The primary mythological source for Rhiannon's story is from a collection of Middle Welsh narrative tales that has come to be called *Pedair Cainc y Mabinogi* or *The Four Branches of the Mabinogi* — often given as *Y Mabinogi* for short. There has been some confusion about the name of this collection of tales, as well as the names of the individual tales themselves since the source manuscripts do not provide titles for any of them. Of the stories collected, only four of them end with the formulaic "and so ends this branch of *Y Mabinogi*", leaving us to conclude that those particular tales are in some way related (Mac Cana, 1992). The word *"mabinogi"* is believed to come from the Welsh *mab,* which means "youth" or "son", and so could potentially mean "Tales of the Youth". This appears to be a Welsh iteration of a type of narrative tradition that relays a hero's youthful adventures, such as we see in the Irish *macnímartha* genre of tales. While the evidence is not entirely conclusive, it is possible that the youthful hero whose exploits unifies these *Four Branches* is none other than Rhiannon's son, Pryderi; we will explore this idea in more depth in chapter four.

The term *"mabinogion"* appears to have been a scribal error in one of the source manuscripts, and when Lady Charlotte Guest translated and published these tales in English for the first time between 1830 and 1840, she did so in multiple volumes which she called *The Mabinogion* — a convention that has remained to this day. Guest included additional medieval Welsh tales in this collection, all taken from the same source manuscripts, but the story cycle properly known as *Y Mabinogi* is formally comprised only of the four *cainc* or branches (Mac Cana, 1992).

The titles given to these branches by Guest are:

The First Branch – *Pwyll Pendefeg Dyfed* (Pwyll, Prince of Dyfed)

The Second Branch – *Branwen ferch Llŷr* (Branwen, Daughter of Llŷr)

The Third Branch – *Manawydan fab Llŷr* (Manawydan, Son of Llŷr)

The Fourth Branch – *Math fab Mathonwy* (Math, Son of Mathonwy)

The additional tales included in the source manuscripts containing the Four Branches and came to be collected with them, but are not part of *Y Mabinogi* proper are:

The Four Native Tales:
Culhwch ac Olwen (*Culhwch and Olwen*)
Lludd a Llefelys (*Lludd and Llefelys*)
Breuddwyd Macsen Wledig (*The Dream of Macsen Wledig*)
Breuddwyd Rhonabwy (*The Dream of Rhonabwy*)

The Three Romances:
Owain, neu Chwedyl Iarlles y Ffynnawn (*Owain, or The Lady of the Fountain*)
Peredur fab Efrawg (*Peredur son of Efrawg*)
Gereint fab Erbin (*Gereint son of Erbin*).

The source manuscripts for these eleven tales are:
Peniarth 6 (The earliest source, dating to about 1250 CE, which is unfortunately fragmentary)
Llyfr Gwyn Rhydderch (The White Book of Rhydderch, dating to around 1350 CE)
Llyfr Goch Hergest (The Red Book of Hergest, dating to around 1400 CE)

While most scholars believe that the tales themselves, as written, may date back as far 1050 CE, there are references to some of the characters in the poems of *The Book of Taliesin* (*Llyfr Taliesin*) which are believed to pre-date *Y Mabinogi*. Further, it is commonly accepted that these tales were redacted from oral tradition, and therefore the stories themselves are likely of much older origin (Davies, 1993). Is it possible that these stories, or at least the seeds of what they wound up becoming, originated in Celtic Pagan British times? Perhaps, but there is no definitive evidence for any direct lineage between them, especially when you consider the timeline involved.

The Iron Age Celts are believed to have come to the British Isles around 500 BCE; the Roman conquest of Britain was complete by 77 CE, and Roman rule lasted until 410 CE. The Roman Empire established Christianity as its official religion in 312 CE, and although there is some evidence of Christianity in the British Isles before this, due to the departure of the Romans and the subsequent invasions of Pagan Saxons, the religion didn't gain a firm foothold until the 6th century (Ross, 1996). As the Pagan Celts themselves held a prohibition against writing any of their sacred teachings down, we do not have any written materials contemporary with ancient Pagan practice in Britain, and since the stories of *Y Mabinogi* were not written down until a good 500 – 700 years later, it is very difficult to find any conclusive proof that these tales have their origins in Pagan British myths.

Rhiannon directly appears in the First and Third Branches of *Y Mabinogi*, playing a larger role in the First Branch than in the Third. She is referenced in the Second Branch, and the Adar Rhiannon—the Birds of Rhiannon—make an appearance. These Otherworldly birds are also mentioned in *Culhwch and Olwen*, and potentially feature, albeit unnamed, in *The Lady of the Fountain*. The Adar Rhiannon are also mentioned in a Welsh Triad whose authenticity is contested, as it is likely the creation of Iolo Morgannwg, the Welsh writer and poet who re-established the Eisteddfod in 1792, and who infamously passed off some of his own writing as translations of old, rare texts thereby casting doubt on the antiquity of all of his writings. Aside from mentions of her son and husbands in other places, including authentic triads from *Trioedd Ynys Prydein (The Triads of the Island of Britain)* and *Llyfr Taliesin (The Book of Taliesin)*, that is the sum of the literary primary source material that we have on Rhiannon. Considering the lack of material culture which attest to her myth or any known cultus directly concerning her, there really isn't very much information to work with, especially in comparison to other deities both within and outside of Celtic cultures.

Let us therefore embark upon a review of these sources so that we can establish a foundational context for understanding Rhiannon and for crafting a devotional practice in her honor. What follows is a straightforward retelling of her stories from all known literary sources; it is recommended that, in addition to these, you read a translation of the tales for yourself as well, as there are details and turns of phrase that cannot be transmitted through a retelling but which can provide important information to the seeker. Even the most direct translations lose something from the original Welsh; the redactors often made use of beautiful linguistic wordplay requiring a fluency in Welsh to appreciate, and therefore non-Welsh readers need to rely upon explanatory notes from the translators in order to understand them.

Chapter Three

Retelling the Myths

Rhiannon in the First Branch

The beginning of the First Branch recounts how Pwyll Pendefig Dyfed, prince of the Welsh kingdom of Dyfed, slighted Arawn, king of the Otherworldly kingdom of Annwn. In order to redress this insult, Pwyll and Arawn changed places with each other, and each noble ruled in the stead--and with the visage--of the other. At the end of a year spent in the guise of Arawn, ruling his kingdom wisely and respecting Arawn's marriage bed by not sleeping with the other king's unsuspecting wife, Pwyll defeated an enemy of Arawn that the Otherworldly king battled every year at a ford. Thus gaining Arawn's gratitude and friendship, Pwyll was given the name Pen Annwn (Chief of Annwn) and returned to Dyfed with many gifts to find that Arawn had ruled well in his place, and brought great prosperity to his kingdom.

Sometime later, after a feast at his court in Arberth, Pwyll and his men visit a nearby hill where, it was said, any noble who sat upon it would either see a wonder or be beaten by many blows. Unconcerned for his safety, and desiring to experience a wonder, Pwyll and his retinue make for the hill, called Gorsedd Arberth. When all are settled and seated, they are met with the sight of a veiled and golden horsewoman astride a tall and pale white horse; she rides along the road that passes in front of the hill, and her mount appears to be walking at a slow and steady pace. Pwyll is intrigued by this stranger, and sends one of his men after her to find out who she is. Thinking that her slow pace would permit him to catch up with her on foot, Pwyll's man runs after her, but he is unable to reach the horse and rider. He returns to the court to get the fastest horse available, but no matter how hard he rides, the horsewoman remains out of reach, and at last he gives up. Pwyll and his men return the next day with their fastest horse, hoping to encounter the mysterious rider once more. She appears almost immediately, again seeming to move at a slow and steady pace, but she again evades Pwyll's man; the harder he pushed his horse, the further away she became even though she never altered her pace. Undeterred, Pwyll and his retinue return the next day, and this time it is Pwyll who pursues Rhiannon on his own horse; just as before, the apparently slow-moving white horse and its rider remain out of reach regardless of how quickly they were pursued. Finally, Pwyll called out to Rhiannon:

"For the sake of the man you love most, wait for me."
"I will wait gladly," she said, "and it would have been better for the horse if you had asked that a while ago!" (Davies 2007, pg. 10)

Drawing her horse to a halt, Pwyll immediately catches up with Rhiannon who draws back her veil. Pwyll thinks to himself that he had never seen so beautiful a woman, and asks who she is and where she is going. She gives him her name, saying:

I am Rhiannon, daughter of Hyfaidd Hen, and I am to be given to a husband against my will. But I have never wanted any man, because of my love for you. And I still do not want him, unless you reject me. And it is to find out your answer on the matter that I have come. (Davies 2007, p. 11)

Captivated, Pwyll responds that if he could choose from any woman in the world, he would choose no one but Rhiannon. Gladdened, Rhiannon arranges to meet with Pwyll at her father's court a year hence, where their wedding feast would be lain and the two of them would be married. As promised, Pwyll and his retinue arrive a year later to the Otherworldly court of Hyfaidd

Hen, and the joyous feast commences, with Rhiannon and Pwyll seated side by side in their place of honor.

During the course of the merrymaking, a man approaches the bride and groom and asks a boon of Pwyll; overcome with goodwill, Pwyll immediately agrees to give the stranger anything within his power to give. Unfortunately, the man is no stranger to Rhiannon, as it is her former suitor Gwawl, who immediately asks for the hand of Rhiannon and the wedding feast besides. Forced, now, to keep the word he had too readily given in front of the entire gathering, Rhiannon takes Pwyll to task for his impulsiveness:

> "Be silent for as long as you like," said Rhiannon. "Never has a man been more stupid than you have been.'" (Davies 2007, pg. 12)

She then turns to Gwawl and informs him that the feast had been laid by her and gifted to the visitors from Dyfed, so it was not Pwyll's to give; however, should Gwawl return in a year's time, she would have another feast waiting and she would become his wife. Gwawl agrees and departs, leaving Rhiannon to comfort the devastated Pwyll. She gives to him a magical bag and a set of instructions and sends him on his way, counseling him to follow her directions exactly so they might yet become married with Pwyll's honor still intact. Promising to do so, Pwyll takes his leave of Rhiannon.

A year later, Pwyll returns to the court of Hyfaidd Hen. A new wedding feast is underway in honor of Rhiannon and Gwawl. Disguised as a beggar, Pwyll approaches the seats of honor and makes a petition for a boon from Gwawl. Cautiously, Gwawl replies that he would give what he could within reason, and Pwyll replies that all he desires is for his bag to be filled up with food from the feast. Eyeing the small bag proffered by Pwyll, Gwawl airily agrees to the boon, and gestures to the servants to fill the bag with food. However, this being Rhiannon's magical bag, no matter how much food is placed into it, it never becomes full. Gwawl's demeanor transforms from smug to concerned as he watches almost the entirety of his feast disappearing into the never-sated bag. Concerned there would not be enough food to feed his guests, Gwawl asks, "Will your bag ever be full?" To which Pwyll replies:

> "Never... no matter what is put in it, unless a nobleman endowed with land and territory and power gets up and treads down the food in the bag with both feet and says 'Enough has been put in here.'." (Davies 2007, pg.14)

Hastily, Gwawl rises up to do just that, and the moment he puts both feet in the bag, Pwyll pulls the sack up over Gwawl's head, then ties it securely shut. Trapped within the bag, Gwawl pleads for help as Pwyll's warriors emerge from hiding and begin kicking the sack about, thereby birthing a new game called "the badger in the bag." Rhiannon and her father are mortified by the ignoble treatment, and call upon Pwyll to bring his men to order. Once done, Rhiannon sets the terms for Gwawl's release, requiring him to give up his claim on her and to vow that he will seek no redress for the indignities suffered at Pwyll's hands. Gwawl agrees to these terms and is released, freeing Pwyll to finally wed Rhiannon and to enjoy the wedding feast.

The couple sleep together that night, and spend a second day in feasting, during which a humble and cautious Pwyll bestowed gifts upon all who asked for them. On the third day they departed for Pwyll's lands, taking residence at his court in Arberth. Rhiannon builds a reputation as a very generous queen, bestowing rich gifts upon courtiers and proving herself a model of hospitality. The couple are very happy, but after three years of marriage without an heir, Pwyll's advisors begin to suggest that he take another wife. He refuses to do so, asking them to let the matter rest for another year as much may yet happen. And indeed, before that year is over, Rhiannon gives birth to a son.

On the night of his birth, six nurses are sent into Rhiannon's chambers to watch over the mother and child, but one by one, they each fall asleep. Awaking before dawn, they realize to their horror that the baby is gone; search as they might, he is nowhere to be found. Fearing they would be put to death for their negligence, the nurses devise a plan to save themselves, knowing that the word of all six of them would win out against the word of Rhiannon. Taking and killing several stag-hound puppies, the nurses smear the blood on the sleeping Rhiannon's face and hands, and arrange the bones all around her. When Rhiannon awakens and asks for her son, the nurses reply that she shouldn't be asking them for him, that they tried and tried to stop her from destroying the baby, but she was too strong and overpowered them. Rhiannon replies that she knows this is a lie, and that they needn't be afraid—that they should tell the truth about what happened and she would ensure that no harm would come to them; but they would not be moved from their course.

As word of the incident spreads throughout the land, Pwyll's advisers beseech him to divorce Rhiannon because of the terrible thing she had done, but Pwyll refuses, preferring instead to punish her. Rhiannon, meanwhile, had gathered her own group of advisors, who recommended that she accept the punishment from Pwyll, rather than try to argue against the six nurses. She agrees to do so, and her punishment was this: for seven years she is to sit every day on a mounting block outside of Arberth's gate, where she is to tell the story of how she destroyed her newborn child to anyone who approached. Additionally, she was to offer any newcomer a ride to the court on her back, and all of this she did, although very few visitors took her up on the offer.

While all of this is going on, Teyrnon Twryf Lliant, the lord of nearby Gwent Is Coed, is vexed with an ongoing problem. Every year on May Eve, or Calan Mai, his fine white mare births a beautiful foal, and every year that foal mysteriously disappears without a trace that same night. Tired of losing such beautiful animals year after year, Teyrnon decides on this May Eve to bring the pregnant horse inside so that he can keep watch over her. When night falls, she gives birth to a beautiful foal, and just as it stands for the first time, an enormous clawed arm reaches through the window and grabs hold of the newborn's mane, seeking to spirit it away.

Teyrnon saves the horse by cleaving the monstrous arm off with his sword so that both foal and claw fall back into the house. He hears a horrible scream outside, and gives chase to the wounded creature as it attempts to escape into the night. Teyrnon doesn't get far before he remembers that he left the door open, and upon returning to ensure that the horses would not escape, discovers a newborn baby swaddled in silk brocade lying on the threshold of his home. He brings the child to his wife, with whom he has had no children, and the two decide to raise the boy as their own after she notes that his clothing clearly mark him as coming from noble lineage. They name the child Gwri Wallt Euryn, (Blooming Golden Hair) because of his blond hair.

Gwri was a strong child who grew incredibly quickly; by the time he was one, he was as developed as a three year old, and when he turned two, he looked and acted more like a six year old. By the time he turned four, he was pestering the grooms to permit him to ride a horse. Teyrnon's wife suggested that the boy be given the horse that Teyrnon had saved on the night he found Gwri; he agreed, and asked her to give it to the boy herself. It was about this time that Teyrnon became aware of the plight and punishment of Rhiannon, and he became filled with compassion for her loss. He then looked to Gwri, and for the first time realized the strong resemblance the boy had to Pwyll, who was known to Teyrnon through once having been Pwyll's vassal.

After conferring with his wife, they decide to make a trip to

Pwyll's court the very next day in order to restore the boy to his family. When they arrive at the gate, they encounter Rhiannon sitting at the mounting block. She introduces herself to them and, as required, offers to carry each of them in turn to Pwyll's court. Everyone refused to allow Rhiannon to carry them, and together entered the court where a feast was being lain in celebration of Pwyll's return from touring the lands around Dyfed. During the feast,Teyrnon recounted the story of finding the golden-haired child, and turning to Rhiannon he said, "This is your son, my lady. And whoever told lies against you did you wrong." (Davies 2007, pg. 20)

Rhiannon replied, "what a relief from my anxiety if that were true!" and it is from this utterance that Pryderi, from the word *pryder,* meaning "anxiety", received his name from Rhiannon (Davies, 2007). Pwyll and Rhiannon are so overcome with gratitude for the way the boy had been raised by Teyrnon, they make assurances that Dyfed will forever support Teyrnon and his lands. They also offered rich rewards, strong horses, and hunting dogs—all of which Teyrnon refused. Pryderi was given as a foster child to Pendaran Dyfed, a wise member of Pwyll's court, and the boy preternaturally grew into adulthood. After Pywll passes away, Pryderi takes over the seven cantrifs of Dyfed, along with fourteen more, and rules them all well. He eventually takes a bride, a woman named Cigfa.

Rhiannon in the Second Branch

Rhiannon does not appear directly in the Second Branch, but her influence in the story is both deeply felt and memorable. A great war breaks out when the king of Britain, Bendigeidfran, or Bran the Blessed, brings an army to Ireland in order to rescue his sister Branwen from the mistreatment she is suffering at the hands of her husband Matholwch, the king of Ireland. The devastation resulting from this war leaves Ireland populated only by five pregnant women who each give birth to sons, and together they repopulate the island and establish Ireland's five provinces. Of the warriors who came from Britain, also known as the Island of the Mighty, only seven survivors return. Branwen, whose young son is killed in the maelstrom, regards the devastation on both sides of the conflict, dies of a broken heart, and is buried in a four-sided grave on the island of Anglesey.

Bran himself is struck with a poisoned spear during the battle, and before he dies, instructs his men to cut off his head and to bring it to White Hill in London, where they are to bury it facing France. This act is immortalized in a Welsh Triad as one of the Three Fortunate Concealments, for as long as Bran's head is buried there, its talismanic power would ensure that Britain could never be conquered by anyone from across the sea. A complementary Triad is that of the Three Unfortunate Disclosures, which relates how King Arthur himself had the head of Bran removed from White Hill because he thought it was unseemly that anyone but he, Arthur, himself should protect the Island of Britain.

However, before the burial of the head, the seven survivors of the war—who counted among them Pryderi son of Rhiannon, and Manawydan son of Llŷr and brother to Bran and Branwen — brought the head with them to Bran's court at Harlech, following their king's instructions. When they arrived and sat at the feast that had been laid out for them, the Adar Rhiannon (the Birds of Rhiannon) began to sing, as Bran foretold:

> As soon as they began to eat and drink, three birds came and began to sing them a song, and all the songs they had heard before were harsh compared to that one. They had to gaze far out over the sea to catch sight of the birds, yet their song was clear as if the birds were there with them. (Davies 2007, p. 33)

Thus attended, the band of men feasted together for seven years, with Bran's head never becoming corrupted; it kept them company the same as it had when it was still upon their king's body. After seven years in Harlech, they departed for Gwales where there was a royal household high above the sea. There, the seven men along with Bran's head, dwelt together for eighty years. All of their needs were met, all of the sorrows of what they had experienced faded away and were forgotten, and they spent that time filled with great joy, with none of them aging and the head of Bran never knowing decay. The group became known as The Assembly of the Noble Head, and it is only when one of their number opened the door Bran had warned them against opening and they looked out towards Cornwall that their memories returned, and they were overcome with sorrow for all that they had lost. They immediately took up Bran's head, which would only remain uncorrupted while the door was closed, and made for London, burying it at White Hill as he had instructed.

Rhiannon in the Third Branch

The story of the Third Branch picks up immediately where the Second Branch leaves off, with the burial of Bran's head in London having been accomplished. Pryderi son of Pwyll and Rhiannon, and Manawydan son of Llŷr had become fast friends. With their memories restored and eighty years having passed, Manawydan lamented that he had nowhere now to go. As the brother of Bran, Manawydan had a claim to the throne of the Island of the Mighty, which had been usurped by his cousin Caswallon during the events of the Second Branch; however, Manawydan chose not to challenge him, lest a new war begin. By not claiming his birthright, Manawydan was counted as one of the Three Undemanding Chieftains, another of the Triads of the Island of Britain.

Pryderi invites his friend to come to Dyfed with him, and along with offering him rule over the seven cantrefs he had inherited from his father Pwyll, he also offers him the hand of the now-widowed Rhiannon. Manawydan decides to visit Dyfed with his friend, and agrees to meet Rhiannon there.

When the men arrive in Arberth, they find that a great feast had been readied for them by Rhiannon and Pryderi's wife Cigfa. Rhiannon and Manawydan sit to talk with each other, and the son of Llŷr is overcome with tenderness for her, thinking he had never encountered such a well-spoken and beautiful woman. Manawydan tells Pryderi that he agrees to his friend's proposal that he marry Rhiannon, and upon learning of the offer, Rhiannon readily agrees to the union. The two are wed that very night.

Soon after the wedding of Manawydan and Rhiannon, Pryderi visits Caswallon at his court in Oxford to pay homage to the king. Upon his return to Dyfed, there is a holy day feast at the main court in Arberth; between courses of food, and along with other feasters attending the celebration, Rhiannon, Manawydan, Pryderi, and Cigfa climb the Gorsedd Arberth, the same hill from which Pwyll first spied Rhiannon on her horse many years ago. Once the four were seated upon the hill, they heard a terrible noise and a blanket of mist descended upon them; it was so thick they could not see each other. Suddenly the mist disappeared and everything became bright again, and with the return of the light the four looked around and saw that every person, every domesticated animal, every dwelling place, and every sign of life aside from them had completely disappeared.

They searched everywhere in the court and eventually searched throughout the countryside, and found that, aside from wild animals, the four of them were utterly alone. After working through the provisions at hand, the two couples sustained themselves by hunting and fishing, spending two contented years together, before deciding that they no longer wished to live alone in this way. Upon Manawydan's suggestion, the four traveled to England, which had not been affected by the strange magic that had rendered Dyfed uninhabited, and in the town of Hereford, took up the craft of saddle making to sustain themselves. Their saddles were so excellently crafted and in such high demand, that the other saddlers banded together and decided they were going to kill them. Warned of this threat, Pryderi suggests that they kill those who were going to come after them, but Manawydan grew worried about their reputations, and counseled that it would be better for the group to leave town and take up a new craft elsewhere.

Following Manawydan's advice, the four take up residence in a new place and begin to create shields of incredible quality. The demand for these shields was so great that the local shield makers became furious and decided to kill the four of them for taking all of their business. Once more warned, Pryderi again suggests that they should go after their enemies and kill them first, but Manawydan expresses concern that Caswallon would hear of it and come after them with his army, and so the four again uproot and move to a new town. This time, they decide to become shoemakers, hoping that any competition would be too meek to try to come after them. Manawydan teaches the others how to make shoes out of fine Spanish leather, and himself learns how to guild the buckles for the shoes—earning himself the reputation of being one of the Three Golden Shoemakers of the Island of the Mighty. However, the group was once more threatened by the other shoemakers whose profits they were impacting. Pryderi again expressed that they should kill those who would try to kill them, but Manawydan's mild nature was once more victorious, and upon his advice that they return to Dyfed and leave England altogether, the four of them do just that.

After a long journey that brought them back to Arberth, the group began to hunt for their food once more, spending a year contentedly in this way. One morning, Manawydan and Pryderi gather their dogs to go hunting when they notice several of them run ahead of the group and into a thicket, only to return with their hair standing on end in terror. The two men investigate the area for themselves, and discover a pure white wild boar hiding there. Along with their now-emboldened dogs, Pryderi and Manawydan give chase until the boar and the dogs run into a strange and enormous towering fort that had never before existed where it now stood. The two men climb the hill upon which the fort had been built, waiting for the dogs to return. But after some time had passed and they did not hear a sound coming from within the fort, Pryderi decides he is going to go inside to find the dogs.

Always cautious, Manawydan counsels against this action, concluding that whoever had built the fort was also the same person who had put a spell on the land. Pryderi insists that he will not abandon his dogs, and ignoring his friend's advice, he enters alone. He soon discovers that the fort is completely empty; there is no sign of habitation, of his dogs, or of the boar. What he does notice, however, is a well at the center of the space, ornamented with fine marble work. Hanging over the edge of the well was a finely wrought golden bowl which was suspended from four chains that extended so high up into the sky that Pryderi could not see where they ended. Drawn to the beauty of this bowl, Pryderi reached out to grab it with both hands and was immediately frozen into place, unable to speak; he could neither move his feet, nor could he release the bowl.

Unaware of his friend's fate, Manawydan waited for him outside until almost evening, finally returning alone to the court at Arberth. Noticing his solitary state, Rhiannon inquired after her son and the dogs, and Manawydan explained what had transpired. Scolding him as a faithless friend, Rhiannon set out to find the mysterious fort for herself, seeking to rescue Pryderi. Upon discovering the gate of the fortress left open, Rhiannon entered to find her son still holding onto the golden bowl, completely immobilized. In an attempt to free him, Rhiannon grabbed hold of the bowl herself and was immediately rendered silent and paralyzed as well. The two stood there motionless until night fell, and as had happened on Gorsedd Arberth many years before, they heard a terrible noise and a blanket of thick mist fell upon the tower before it—with them inside—disappeared.

When Cigfa and Manawydan discovered that they were alone, Pryderi's wife was overcome with grief and worry until Manawydan assured her that he would not seek to dishonor her in any way. As they had lost their hunting dogs and could not obtain food for themselves, the pair made for England, with Manawydan setting up shop to be a shoemaker once again. Cigfa argued that this craft was both below his station and his skill set, but he insisted that this was the work he wanted to pursue. They lived in the town where they settled for a year until, as before, the local shoemakers began to plot against them. This time it was Cigfa who urged Manawydan to act against their persecutors, but he decided it was better for them to return to Dyfed, and they did.

Bringing with him a bundle of wheat, Manawydan and Cigfa settled in Arberth once more, and he learned how to fish and trap wild animals for their food. He also began to till the soil, and planted three fields' worth of wheat. When the time of the Harvest arrived, he visited his fields and found that they were ripe, and he committed to reap the first of his fields the next day. However, when he arrived in the early morning, he found that the entire field had been decimated and every stalk of wheat had been cut down and the grain carried away. Concerned, he checked on his second field, and found that it was ripe and intact and committed to reap it the next day. When he arrived the next morning, he discovered that the second field had now become emptied of grain, and he lamented his terrible fortune while also recognizing that whoever was responsible for the destruction of his fields also had set the enchantment upon the land and had carried away Rhiannon and Pryderi.

Discovering that his third field was ripe and still intact, Manawydan returned home to gather his weapons and to keep watch over the fields during the night, with the hope that he could protect his harvest and discover who had been acting against him. Thus armed and vigilant, Manawydan returned to the last field. Around midnight, he heard an incredibly loud sound, and suddenly an entire army of mice descended upon the field, breaking every stalk and carrying away every head of grain. Manawydan tried in vain to stop them, but there were too many and he could not grab hold of them before it was too late and the field was bare. He was able, at last, to capture one little mouse who was fatter and slower than the rest; he placed it in one of his gloves and tied it up so the mouse could not escape. He brought it back to court with him and told Cigfa that he intended to hang the mouse as a thief the next day. She at first tried to dissuade him, as it was below his status to bother with such a lowly creature, but he was adamant and since she could come up with no other reason for him to release the mouse, she relented.

Manawydan then made for the Gorsedd Arberth, and at the very top of the hill, he began to create a makeshift gallows by pressing two forks into the ground. As he was doing so, he caught sight of a cleric approaching him—the first person, other than his three companions, that he had seen in Dyfed in seven years. The two exchanged greetings and the cleric said he had come from England and was passing through Arberth. When the cleric asked what Manawydan was doing, he replied that he was going to hang the mouse as a thief in accordance with the law. The cleric tried to convince Manawydan to let the mouse go, even offering him money, but he would not, and so the cleric continued on.

Manawydan was affixing a crossbeam over the two forks when a priest approached him and asked what he was doing. He again replied that he was going to hang the mouse as a thief and refused to be paid off or convinced otherwise by the priest, who likewise continued on his way. Manawydan began to tie a rope around the neck of the mouse when he became aware of a bishop and his retinue approaching. Like the others, the bishop tried to convince Manawydan to release the mouse or else allow him to pay money for it; Manawydan refused. The bishop tried again, offering a much larger sum of money, but Manawydan would not be moved. The bishop then promised that in return for the release of the mouse, he would give him the seven horses that had accompanied his retinue as well as the seven bags of riches on each of the seven horses besides. Once more, Manawydan refused.

Finally and desperately, the bishop asked what Manawydan's price was to release the mouse, to which he replied, "The release of Rhiannon and Pryderi." The bishop assured him he would have that, but it was not enough for Manawydan, who also demanded that the enchantment be lifted from Dyfed. That too was promised to him, but it was still not enough as Manawydan wanted to know who the captive mouse was. The other man replied that she was his pregnant wife, and with prompting from Manawydan, the "bishop" explained everything:

> "I am Llwyd son of Cil Coed, and it is I who placed the enchantment on the seven cantrefs of Dyfed, and I did so to avenge Gwawl son of Clud out of friendship for him; and I took revenge on Pryderi because Pwyll Pen Annwfn played Badger in the Bag with Gwawl son of Clud and he did so unwisely at the court of Hyfaidd Hen. And having heard that you were living in the land, my retinue came to me and asked me to turn them into mice so they could destroy your corn... the third night my wife and the ladies of the court came to me and asked me to transform them too, and I did that." I believe the quotation marks should remain here as they appear in the text as well; the character is speaking. (Davies 2007, p. 45)

Llwyd asked for his wife to be released once more, but Manawydan wisely refused to do so until he received assurances that there would be no other spell ever cast upon Dyfed; that there would be no further vengeance taken against Rhiannon and Pryderi, or any on him because of what had occurred; and that Rhiannon and Pryderi be returned to him before he released the mouse. Praising the good bargain that Manawydan had made, especially that it avoided any further action against Manawydan himself, Llwyd agreed to all of the conditions. Rhiannon and Pwyll appeared, and they gratefully embraced each other, and the enchantment over Dyfed was lifted, with all of the people, homesteads, and livestock returned to their proper places. Manawydan released the mouse to her husband who changed her back to her proper form with his magic wand.

Satisfied that all things had been restored to their proper place, Manawydan made one last inquiry about the nature of the captivity that had been endured by Pryderi and Rhiannon. Llwyd replied:

"Pryderi had the gate-hammers of my court around his neck, while around hers, Rhiannon had the collars of the asses after they had been hauling hay. And that was their imprisonment. (Davies 2007, p. 46)

And so concludes the Third Branch of the *Mabinogi*.

Rhiannon in *Culhwch and Olwen*

As with the Second Branch, Rhiannon does not directly appear in this story, which is the oldest prose Arthurian tale; its earliest redaction is believed to date to somewhere in the 10th or 11th centuries CE (Bromwich, 1992). The tale, in brief, recounts the exploits of Arthur and his knights on behalf of his cousin Culhwch who has fallen in love with Olwen, the daughter of the giant Ysbaddaden Bencawr who is fated to die when his daughter marries. Because of this, Ysbaddaden sets a series of incredibly difficult and seemingly impossible feats before Culhwch and his allies, all of which needed to be accomplished before the giant would grant permission for the marriage to occur. One of these requirements was to obtain for him the Birds of Rhiannon, "they that wake the dead and lull the living to sleep" (Davies 2007, p.196), so that they will sing for Ysbaddaden on the night of the wedding, which would also be the last night of his life. Ultimately, with the help of his warriors and from Arthur himself, Culhwch is able to complete all of the challenges set before him by Olwen's father. Ysbaddaden keeps his word, and gives his daughter to Culhwch; the giant is then beheaded by one of Arthur's men, who takes over his lands and holdings.

Rhiannon in the Welsh Triads

Believed to be a creation of Iolo Morgannwg, rather than an authentic triad, this is nevertheless included here for the sake of completion as it is often referenced in regards to Rhiannon:

There are three things which are not often heard: the song of the birds of Rhiannon, a song of wisdom from the mouth of a Saxon, and an invitation to a feast from a miser. (*Trioedd y Cybydd*, cited in Guest, p.209)

The Mythic Landscape

Y Mabinogi is filled with references to the contemporary landscape of the medieval redactors, perhaps as a reflection of the nationalistic spirit of this transitional time in Welsh history—a deliberate effort on the part of the Welsh to preserve their culture in the face of losing their national autonomy during the Anglo-Norman conquest. The tales may have reminded the Britons of a time when they were independent kingdoms, at times unified under the aegis of a high king, especially in times of strife and against the threat of invasion. Happily, many of the sites mentioned in the text still exist and are accessible enough to be directly experienced today.

Whereas many sites are named directly in the narrative of the Four Branches, and there are many inferences through onomastic tales which explain why a place bears a particular name, it is still difficult to discern what came first, the name or the tale. Perhaps some of the sites are included because they carry faint mythic memories of cult sites sacred to a particular deity, or perhaps the tale came afterwards, in an attempt to provide a retroactive explanation for why things were named or built, or why certain artifacts or ruins exist long after their original uses had been forgotten over time. Either way, the energies of the tales have come to rest in particular landscape areas, and many modern locals are aware of folk traditions which surround the sites, even those which have not been directly recorded in the myths themselves. Further, the study of Welsh toponyms or place names is a worthwhile pursuit, as it can deepen one's understanding of how very important was the land of Wales itself to its mythic heritage.

The main setting of the First and Third Branches is Dyfed, an historical kingdom believed to have once been the territory of the Demetae, a Brythonic Celtic tribe from whom the region got its name. In *Y Mabinogi*, Dyfed is comprised of seven cantrefs, a political unit used in medieval Wales that refers to an area made up of one hundred settlements (from the Welsh *cant* (hundred) and *tref* (town)) (Bollard, 2006). Dyfed is in south-west Wales and its territory was roughly comprised of today's Pembrokeshire and part of Carmarthenshire (Davies, 2007). Arberth in Dyfed was the chief court of Pwyll, and later also that of Pryderi and Manawydan. It is here that Rhiannon gave birth to Pryderi, and where she was sentenced to sit at the gates and offer travelers a ride on her back as penance for her unjust accusation of infanticide. Near to the court was Gorsedd (meaning "tumulus" or "burial mound", or else "throne" or "court") Arberth (Bollard, 2006), the mysterious mound from which Pwyll first encountered Rhiannon, and from where the enchantment of Dyfed in the Third Branch both came down and was lifted.

It is believed that Arberth once existed where modern-day

Narberth now stands. There, one can visit the ruins of a Norman motte and bailey castle, believed to have been built in the 12th century CE. While this date is problematic for this having been the court of Pwyll and Rhiannon, the Normans were known for building castles upon older sites, likely because both were chosen for their strategic position. Indeed, not far from the ruins of Castle Narberth, there is a place called Camp Hill which features the remains of an Iron Age enclosure; this appears to be the location most favored to have once been Gorsedd Arberth, and it is the setting for the introduction to this book (Bollard, 2006).

Chapter Four

Rhiannon and Divinity

With what is directly known about Rhiannon from primary source materials as our foundation, we can now work to seek a greater understanding of her. We shall do so through an exploration of her symbols from a cultural perspective, through an examination of her trans-cultural associations with potentially related divinities, by identifying the international folk motifs that are present in her tales, and by investigating the nature of the relationships she has with other mythic characters. Although this kind of analysis is, by nature, much more subjective than any face value reading of her mythos, the tools and process are based in solid academic and scholastic inquiry and so can be used to build a bridge of connection to Rhiannon with some degree of objectivity.

Although Rhiannon is neither directly identified as a divinity in the text of *Y Mabinogi*, nor have we discovered to date anything in the archaeological record that proves that the Pagan Britons worshiped a figured named Rhiannon, the question of whether or not she is a Goddess can be addressed through a thorough exploration of older figures in Celtic tradition who are clearly attested to be divinities and with whom she appears to have correspondence and relationship. There are several streams of investigation to consider, and while their interrelatedness appears to present as a tangled skein, when taken collectively, the areas of differentiation and those of redundancy paint a picture which permits us to conclude that Rhiannon may well be a complex divinity who embodies and inherits a rich corpus of tradition in her person, albeit subtextually. How much the contemporary medieval Welsh audience may have recognized these aspects of her character as having ancient Pagan roots is unknown, and perhaps beside the point, although there are some medieval writings where Pagan and Christian traditions are depicted together quite comfortably.

Britain had been solidly Christian for at least 500 years when the Four Branches began to be written down, and yet the stories are overflowing with magic and supernatural beings. Sojourns into the Otherworld—strongly believed to be a remnant of Pagan British cosmology—are common, and references to pre-Christian religious practices are made in the text without judgment. Although it may seem odd that a Christian society would have been so accepting of the supernatural, medieval Welsh culture embraced these fantastic story elements and did not appear to find any contradiction in this. There is a phenomenon observed through the analysis of myth called "reverse euhemerization" which posits that larger than life heroes or supernatural beings found in myths, such as fairy women or giants, had once been divinities whose stature—literally and metaphorically—diminished over time. It is possible therefore that characters in Welsh Mythology who have associations with the Otherworld were once divinities, a theory which helps us better understand Rhiannon as a Goddess, rather than solely as an example of the international folk motif of the Fairy Bride.

In these tales, the Indigenous Otherworld of Britain—called Annwn or Annwfn in Welsh mythos, and believed to mean "Un-World" or "Very Deep"—seems to exist side by side with the human world, and the boundaries between them sometimes become blurred. There are subtextual markers throughout the tales which would have functioned to allow the contemporary medieval audience to understand that the Otherworld was near, or that the threshold into the magical world has been crossed. One of the functions of myth is that it presents a cosmological template both for the society which birthed it and for the place each individual has within that society; it defines the sacred order of things and serves as a cautionary tale for what happens when something or someone upsets the balance and moves outside of this order. The Otherworld therefore provides a mythic arena within which characters and situations that are outside of the constraints of society can be explored. This is important because it is safer to explore what happens when a woman chooses to circumvent her family's choice of a mate for her, for example, when she is a Fairy Woman, because she is already outside of the natural order and her choices, therefore, do not serve to inspire contemporary women to make the same choices. If going outside of the natural order of things is an action reserved for supernatural beings, no ordinary woman could do the same without dire consequences.

There needs to be a balance with this perspective, however. The idealization of women or depictions of women holding power or privileges not known to contemporary medieval women are often attributed to an earlier narrative strata representing a time period featuring different cultural norms when it comes to women. The Irish Queen Medb and the Welsh Arianrhod are examples of this; they are both rulers who display an enormous amount of personal agency and autonomy, to a degree that a regular medieval woman would never know. While some scholars, like Proinsias Mac Cana, suggest this inconsistency may be proof of pagan Celtic mythological remnants entering the narrative through oral folk tradition, others, like Joanne Findon, warn against making broad generalizations of this kind. She argues that seeing Goddesses in all Celtic depictions of women act to further marginalize the depiction of real women rather than to empower them:

Common among scholars of Celtic literature to assume strength and prominence of female characters... must represent the residue of an earlier mythic discourse... disproportionate emphasis on mythological analysis therefore quest for survivals from a presumed base overshadow the possible concerns of the text's 'present' – that is, the time(s) in which it was composed and transmitted. The result is a radical dehistoricizing of the text, its characters, and concerns. Women are not read as themselves but as archetypes in disguise, bearing the weight of a mythic past that can be glimpsed only dimly at best. (Findon, 1997, pg. 8)

The magical, Otherworldly origins of Rhiannon might have been enough to make her stand out in the Four Branches, but her actions are themselves remarkable even if she were but a mortal queen of her time. It may well be that her boldness and autonomy are a memory of a former social paradigm where women held more power. If she herself comes from the Otherworld of a past or fading culture, her disempowerment upon marriage and childbirth might be symbolic of what happens when women are absorbed into the new order—one of patriarchal constraint and societal limitation for women. Yet:

...while Rhiannon is evidently aware of the inequalities of contemporary society, she has not embarked upon a struggle against it so much as within it. This is a crucial distinction since unlike Aranrhod, who refuses to accept social patterns, Rhiannon seeks to improve her lot by working with the system. Thus Rhiannon does not flee from the obligation to marry but simply chooses a type of man to suit her best. (Winward, 1997)

Determining which characters possess attributes that point to their past divinity and which are simply meant to represent inspirational women and men who are powerful in their own right is a task which requires discernment; relying upon only one stream of data can be limiting in this regard. It is therefore important that, in addition to the mythic narrative itself, we take multiple factors into consideration when deciding if a figure is indeed, at the core, a devolved representation of a divinity. The approach I take is one which considers characterization and function in primary source materials, identification of international folk motifs, cultural context, name etymology, the presence of linguistic theonyms, syncretism, material culture in the archaeological record, iconography, and symbolic analysis.

Even with all of these, it is critical to stress that without direct primary proof that a figure is a divinity — for example, a proven archaeological discovery of a devotional altar inscribed with the divinity's name — we cannot say with complete and utter certainty from an academic perspective that the mythic character in question is definitely a god. The standards for accepting a figure as a deity are different, however, when it comes to modern day Neo-Pagan devotional practices; indeed, there are whole magical and religious traditions which have arisen around figures and philosophies of modern cultural origins. There is no question that Rhiannon is greatly beloved and honored as a Goddess by modern devotees around the world regardless of whether she was once worshiped as such by ancient Celtic Britons. The final section of this book suggests ways to build a relationship with, and craft devotional practices around Rhiannon, but for now, let us explore the evidence we do have of Rhiannon's divinity from the context of the culture which birthed her.

Etymology and Linguistics

One of the first clues to Rhiannon's true nature is her very name. Most Celtic scholars agree that Rhiannon is the medieval Welsh reflex of the Old Celtic *Rīgantona, a Gallo-Brittonic Goddess whose name means "Great Queen" or "Divine Queen." In fact, Koch calls *Rīgantona the "preform of the Welsh Rhiannon" (Koch, p. 1490). *Rīgan is the Proto-Celtic word for "queen", which is the etymological root from which the Welsh word *rhiain*, originally meaning "queen", but has come to mean "maiden" or "lady" is derived. *Rīgantona is also believed to be the antecedent of the Irish Goddess Mórrígan whose name also means "Great Queen" or, alternatively, "Phantom Queen" (Beck, 2009). This is the first of several connections that Rhiannon has with the Mórrígan, as we shall see.

Another clue can be found in the terminal deific which is present at the end of Rhiannon's name. The suffix "-on" appears in the names of many Welsh mythological figures including Modron, Mabon, Teyrnon, Gwion, and Gwydion. This is a direct reflex of the "-onos" and "-ona" terminations, meaning "Great" or "Divine", which mark the names of known Gallo-Brittonic deities such as Epona, Sirona, Maponos, and Matrona (Hamp, 1999). Similarly, the "-wen" suffix, which means "white, shining, holy" in Welsh can be found in the names of mythological female characters like Ceridwen, Branwen, and Olwen; the male counterpoint to this is "gwyn", which has the same meaning, and can be seen in the names of Gwyn ap Nudd, and Gwion. The practice carried on into the Christian period, where some Welsh saints' names are constructed with the addition of an honorific prefix "ty", meaning "your."

Connections to Other Goddesses

While Rhiannon is only known to us from the relatively late sources of the Welsh medieval literary tradition, the etymology of her name and her associated symbol sets are shared with older figures who are clearly Goddesses in their own right. While similarities with other divinities are something to note, it in no way implies that these Goddesses are all the same Goddess. There are several possibilities present, several of which may have happened concurrently: 1) That the medieval Rhiannon evolved into her literary form from that of a Celtic British Goddess over centuries of oral tradition. 2) That she is the Welsh reflex of older Celtic Goddesses, possibly from the Continent, which speaks to a Gallo-Brittonic tradition. 3) That she represents a local aspect of a divinity type which is found in many Indo-European cultures, especially those in the Celtic cultural branches. 4) That she is a purely literary character in alignment with several international folk motifs found all over Europe. There are arguments for and against each of these possibilities, and it is impossible to say for sure what the ultimate truth is, based upon the information we currently possess. However, an exploration of the Goddesses which have commonalities of mythos, etymology, and iconography can serve to broaden our understanding of Rhiannon, and deepen our relationship with her.

The Matres and Matronae

One of the richest sources of information about Celtic Goddesses comes to us from continental Europe, where an abundance of epigraphic and iconic evidence supports the existence of a widespread cultus centered on the veneration of Mother Goddesses. Found primarily in Gaul and the Rhineland, and later spreading throughout the Roman Empire to eventually find its way to Britain through the devotion of the Roman soldiers garrisoned there, inscriptions called these Goddesses variously *Matres*, *Matronae*, and *Deae Matronae*—simply, "The Mothers" or "The Divine Mothers." These names are believed to be Latinized forms of the Celtic Gaulish word for mother (*mātīr*)—which itself derives from the Indo-European **mātēr*, as does *mētēr* in Greek and *māter* in Latin (Beck, 2009).

It is challenging to ascertain the cultural origins of this cultus because we don't have clear archaeological evidence of their worship until after the Roman annexation of Germany and Gaul. As the Celts did not commit their sacred things to writing, and it appears that they did not create images of their divinities, it was only in the Gallo-Roman period that we begin to see dedicatory altars to the Mothers as well as syncretic imagery that depicted these Goddesses with some of the iconography of Roman deities. It is generally accepted that while their names derive from a combination of Gaulish and Latin, the oldest epigraphic evidence we have for the Mothers is in Gaulish, which suggests that they were a Celtic religious form rather than a Roman import (Beck, 2009).

The Matronae were typically depicted in triune form, but not in the way some modern Pagans conceptualize the Triple Goddess. These were the Mothers—granters of abundance, fertility, and sovereignty—and their cultus was popular and widespread. While there are many examples of formal devotional shrines and temple stele dedicated to the Matronae and Matres across Europe (with the latter name being preferred in Celtic areas, and the former more common in Germanic territories), the archaeological record has also yielded examples of mass produced Matronae statuary crafted from terra-cotta and other inexpensive materials; it is likely therefore that these deities had also been honored in household shrines (Beck, 2009).

They were often depicted seated, and many featured them wearing distinctive headdresses or rounded bonnets which are believed to reflect the traditional dress of the Germanic Ubii tribe, along with crescent-shaped lunulae necklaces and center-pinned cloaks. Occasionally, the central figure of the three was depicted with their hair down, which is believed to indicate her unwed status. The Mothers held various objects in their laps all of which underscored their roles as granters of fertility and abundance. Some scholars believe that the triads of Goddesses bearing the name Matronae are somewhat different from those who are called Matres. The Matronae appear to be reflective of women who are more mature and hold a higher social authority, like the Roman matrons who are heads of households, and are depicted holding objects that convey abundance within the domestic sphere such as baskets of food, spindles, and bags of coins. The Matres, on the other hand, appear to be concerned more directly and literally with motherhood and child rearing, and are shown nursing infants, holding children, and folding diapers. (Garman, 2008).

These Goddesses are likely not the same figures in all

depictions, as the iconography associated with them appears quite variable, and where there are inscriptions, we can observe that many have been given attributive bynames or epithets that describe the nature, origin, or function of the divinities. For example, Matronae often bear toponyms which connect them to a specific area, ostensibly the area from which they originated, that they serve to embody, and is directly under their care. The bynames have also been used to describe the Goddesses' connection with or authority over different animals, trees, and other natural phenomenon like springs and rivers. Ethnonyms were also used, honoring them as ancestresses of specific tribes, although it is unclear if the tribes were named after their deities or if the Goddesses were given the names of the tribes. Some Matronae are named by their functions, like the Nutrices who feed and care for children, while others are named for the attributes they embody, and still others appear to be tutelary divinities, perhaps hinting at local ancestral worship (Beck, 2009).

It is possible that a folk memory of the worship of these divine mothers persists in Southern Wales where a common appellation for the fairy folk is "Bendith y Mamau"—the Blessings of the Mothers (Hamp, 1999).

Matrona

In singular form, this Goddess was called Matrona, meaning "Divine Mother". This Gaulish deity was likely the personification of the river Marne in France which once bore her name; a Gallo-Roman sanctuary dedicated to Dea Matrona was erected in the 1st century CE near the source of the river at Bellesmes, although votive offerings have been found at this sanctuary which date from the Late Bronze through to the Roman period. As the Marne region is also the area where the distinctive La Tène art style developed in concert with other cultural manifestations that spread through the Continental Celtic and British areas, Koch posits that, "the

Marne country had been the epicenter of the cult of the mother goddess called Matrona, that this cult had originally been linked to the depositional rituals in the river itself, and that it then spread from there—to Britain and the Rhine—with the dominant Marnian culture" (Koch, 2006, p. 1279). This is an important piece of information to consider as we explore roots of Rhiannon's divinity, as we will see.

Although it is uncertain, the cult of Matrona was likely associated with that of the Three Mothers, and references to her have been found in Gaulish and British dedications; her mythos has not survived, however. What is known is that Matrona had a child called Maponos ("Divine Son"), and that this dyad was widely revered by the continental Celts. The Romans came to associate Maponos with Apollo, the perpetual youth, and like his mother, his cultus spanned Northern Europe both in his syncretic and indigenous forms. Maponos was especially revered among Roman soldiers garrisoning Hadrian's Wall, and there is evidence of a concentration of his worship in the north of England, particularly in the area north-west of the Wall (Bromwich, 2006).

Epona

The Gallo-Brittonic Goddess Epona ("Divine Mare") is a unique figure as she is ostensibly the only Celtic deity to have been widely worshiped by the Romans without having been overlain with a Roman deity with similar characteristics and functions, as was the general Roman practice. Her myths have been lost to us, but we know her from devotional inscriptions and cult images found throughout the Roman Empire. In addition to Celtic Gaul, she appears to have been a very popular Goddess in Britain, and we have found devotional images of the Goddess as far north as Hadrian's Wall. She is not considered to have been a pan-Celtic deity; it is rather more likely that her worship spread because she was particularly revered by the Roman cavalry, a large portion of which was made up of Celtic horsemen (Wood, 1997). Despite her soldier following, Epona does not seem to have had a directly martial function, unlike the equine Irish Goddess Macha, who is often discussed in relation to both Epona and Rhiannon.

In addition to formal temples and dedicatory stele, contemporary Roman writings tell us a bit more about the ways that Epona was honored. For example, in his immortal work *The Golden Ass,* Apuleius writes:

[3.27] These thoughts were interrupted by my catching sight of a statue of the goddess Epona seated in a small shrine centrally placed, where a pillar supported the roof-beams in the middle of a stable. The statue had been devotedly garlanded with freshly picked roses.

Of her birth, we have this Roman account from the first century, CE:

Fulvius Stellus hated women and used to consort with a mare and in due time the mare gave birth to a beautiful girl and they named her Epona. She is the goddess that is concerned with the protection of horses. (Plutarch, *Parallela Minora*, p.299)

Some scholars believe that Epona was a specialized Matrona figure (Gruffydd, 1953), set apart by iconography of which there are two main types. The "Side-saddle" type is more common throughout Gaul, and depicts Epona seated peacefully side-saddle on a still or gently moving horse; she is facing forward towards the viewer, while the horse is presented in side-view—typically, right-facing. The "Imperial" type is generally found outside of Gaul but within a Roman context, and shows the Goddess seated (or sometimes standing), and facing forward while flanked by two or four side-view horses; often they face towards the Goddess between them and eat from her hand or from a basket in her lap (Beck, 2009). Depictions of Epona sometimes show her accompanied by a foal whom she often feeds from a cornucopia or other vessel in much the same way the Matronae were often rendered with baskets of food or loaves of bread in their laps; however, unlike these other Divine Mothers, Epona is never shown with a human child.

She is sometimes depicted holding a key, which may point to Epona possessing a psychopomp aspect; that is, she acted to guide the souls of the departed to their rest in the Otherworld, and indeed, she is depicted on funerary stele as well. This perspective is in alignment with the theory that horses, in addition to being symbols of sovereignty in Celtic lands, were also seen as threshold guardians, and were able to cross the boundaries between this world and the next (Ross, 2001). We will explore both of these concepts later on in the text.

Primarily because of their shared equine associations, Rhiannon is generally accepted to be a Welsh reflex of Epona; the two are related but were likely not the same Goddess. That they both can be traced back to the Matronae, albeit by different paths, may be significant, as are the commonalities in some of their symbol sets. There is even one extant inscription where she is referred to in the plural, "Eponabus", in what appears to be a direct mirror of the Matronae (MacCulloch, 1911). Epona exhibits a fertility aspect as represented by the cornucopia or dish of food she sometimes carries, and she was often depicted holding a bag; the latter may be related to the magical bag Rhiannon gives to Pywll which can never be filled to capacity with food, unless a nobleman pushes it down with his feet.

Epona's relationship to sovereignty is also present on several levels. The most obvious is, of course, her status as the Divine Mare and all of the attendant connections to sovereignty that brings. Further, the unhurried pace of Rhiannon's horse when we first meet her in the First Branch appears to correspond with the calm and peaceful depictions of Epona's mount. Finally, in some dedicatory inscriptions, the Goddess is called "Epona Rigani"—the Divine Queen Mare (Koch, 2006). The epithet *Rigani*, meaning "queen", is clearly a connection etymologically to *Rīgantona and, by extension, to Rhiannon herself.

Modron and Mabon

Another thread that connects the Matronae to Rhiannon is Modron, the Welsh reflex of Matrona, whose name also simply means "Divine Mother." Likewise, Modron's son Mabon is a reflex of the divinity Maponus. This Divine Mother-Son dyad appears to be a recurring theme in several Celtic cultures. In addition to Gaulish inscriptions to Matrona and Maponus, and the tales of Modron and Mabon from Welsh narrative tradition, in Ireland we see the pattern manifest in the personages of Boand, who is a river Goddess like Matrona, and her son Oengus Mac ind Óc. His epithet, meaning "Young Son", is thought to have derived from the Old Irish *Maccan Oac*, leading scholars to believe that he too is related to the same Proto-Celtic God as Maponus and Mabon (Hamp, 1999).

Modron is present both directly and indirectly in Welsh tradition, and the evolution of her story can be traced from early Welsh literature to Arthurian legend and through to later Christian hagiographies. Modron features anecdotally in the tale of her son Mabon that appears in the early Welsh story *Culhwch and Olwen,* which is also the earliest extant Arthurian prose tale. In *Culhwch,* we learn that, "Mabon son of Modron, was taken when three nights old from his mother. No one knows where he is, nor what state he's in, whether dead or alive" (Davies 2007, p. 198). The eponymous Culhwch, with the help of his cousin King Arthur and his knights, must find Mabon as part of a Herculean series of quests that must be completed so that Culhwch can marry the woman he loves.

Mabon's imprisonment is further attested in Triad 52 of *Trioedd Ynys Prydein,* which records the following:

Three Exalted Prisoners of the Island of Britain: Llŷr Half-Speech, and Mabon son of Modron, and Gwair son of Geirioedd. (Bromwich, 2006, p. 424)

After a long search, Mabon's whereabouts is discovered and he is freed from the tortures of his prison; he is then able to aid Culhwch in his quest to hunt down a giant boar named Twrch Trwyth. Mabon was the only huntsman in the world who could hunt with a dog so strong it needed a special collar and leash, while on a horse so fast it was as swift as an ocean wave—both of which were necessary to bring down the boar. Mabon is mentioned in several other early Arthurian tales as a member of his court, and is believed to have been integrated into the later Arthurian corpus in the guise of characters named Mabonagrain, Maboun, and Mabuz—all of whom also have story lines associated with imprisonment (Bromwich, 2006).

It is easy to see the parallels between the stories of Mabon and Pryderi: both sons are taken from their mothers as newborns; after their disappearances, no one knows if they are dead or alive, and if alive, their whereabouts are unknown; both Mabon and Pryderi are imprisoned in fortresses, and are punished or made to suffer; they are both hunters and are seen pursuing magical or Otherworldly boars; and they both have connections to dogs and affinities for horses. Celticist W.J. Gruffydd believed that Gwair, one of the three prisoners mentioned in Triad 52, is the same person as Gwri—the name that Teyrnon gave to the infant Pryderi; Gwair also appears as the prisoner mentioned in *The Spoils of Annwn* (Gruffydd, 1953). These similarities do not prove that they are both the same deity, but certainly Mabon and Pryderi are reflexes of each other. "The suspicion is that, like Pryderi, these figures represent localized variants of the Magical Prisoner archetype, all of which perhaps stem back to Mabon ap Modron" (Parker, 2005).

There is a theory that the word *Mabinogi* translates as "Myths

Pertaining to Mabon or Maponos" (Hamp, 1999). Pryderi's connection with Mabon suggests the possibility that he was once the central figure of *Y Mabinogi*; indeed he is the only character who appears in all Four Branches, even if only in a supporting role. We see Pryderi born in the First Branch; come into his manhood as a warrior in the Second Branch; inherit land and title, but share rule of his lands with Manawydan and Rhiannon in the Third Branch; and then finally, fully in his sovereign power in the Fourth Branch, we see Pryderi lose his life to Gwydion in single combat. These are incredibly evocative slivers of what appears to have been a rich heroic cycle that is now lost to us, save for these tantalizing glimpses.

Returning now to Modron, she is mentioned again in Triad 70 of *Trioedd Ynys Prydein*, which enumerates the Three Fair Womb-Burdens of the Island of Britain; the second of which is:

> Owain, son of Urien and Morfudd his sister who were carried together in the womb of Modron, daughter of Afallach. (Bromwich, 2006, pg. 449)

The father of the twins mentioned in the above triad is Urien Rheged, a 6th-century semi-historic warrior-king who ruled the early Northern British kingdom of Rheged; the area today is part of Scotland, but during Urien's reign, it was culturally Brythonic like the region which ultimately became Wales. A story preserved in Peniarth Ms. 147 tells how in Llanferran all of the dogs of the countryside kept gathering on the banks of a river which came to be called "The Ford of Barking" because of the din they raised. No one except Urien was brave enough to investigate this strange phenomenon, and when he arrived at the ford, all he saw was a woman washing in the water. The barking suddenly ended, and Urien, "seized the woman and had his will of her" (Bromwich, 2006, pg. 449). When he was done, she blessed him and revealed to him that she was the daughter of the King of Annwn, and that she had been fated to wash in the river until she was delivered of a son by a Christian man. She implored him to return at the end of the year so that she could give to him their son. He does so, and finds that he has sired both a son and a daughter: Owain, who was a famous Welsh hero, and Morfudd, who was renowned for the devoted love she shared with her husband.

There are several points here to note. The washer woman is not named in this story, but in almost every other sense the tale is identical in detail to Triad 70, allowing us to conclude that she is Modron. She identifies herself as the daughter of the King of Annwn, whose name is Afallach in Triad 70. Afallach is the son of Beli Mawr, a British solar deity married to Dôn, the ostensibly divine ancestress of a lineage of divinities called the Children of Dôn, which included Arianrhod, Gwydion, and Gilfaethwy, whom we know from the Fourth Branch of Y Mabinogi. It appears to have been common for British ruling families of Urien's time to claim lineage from divine or historically significant ancestors. It is meaningful therefore to consider that the family of the historical Urien Rheged claimed descent from Afallach, a fact that exists independently of Triad 70 (Koch, 2006).

The name Afallach means *"Place of Apples"*, and is one of several pieces of lore which connected Modron's father to Ynys Afallon, the Otherworldly Island of Apples, also called Avalon. Because of this we can confidently say that at the very least Modron would have been recognized by the contemporary medieval audience as a fairy woman. Her connection to Avalon goes even deeper. In later Arthurian tales, King Uriens of the North is married to Arthur's sister, and she bears him a son whose name, depending on the provenance of the tale, is given either as Owain or Yvaine—both great Arthurian heroes. And what is the name of Urien's wife, who is also Owain's mother, and Arthur's sister? Morgan le Fay—a powerful healer and wielder of magic, who also appears to be a reflex of the Goddess Modron. And while their names are not cognate, as Morgan is an

Old Welsh name meaning *"Sea-born"*, both Morgan and Modron are powerful figures with strong water associations (Bromwich, 2006).

Another female figure associated with water is represented by the international folk motif known as the Washer at the Ford; this motif has iterations present both in narrative tradition as well as the folk beliefs of almost every Celtic culture. It typically manifests as a Goddess or Otherworldly woman washing the bloody clothing or limbs of a warrior who is fated to die in battle. While this existent story of Urien doesn't have the death-omen component, and seems to rather be about the granting of Sovereignty through sexual congress with a Goddess (which often occurs at liminal places like river banks, and at liminal times like dusk or Samhain), there is a very similar tale from Irish tradition that incorporates both themes (Bromwich, 2006). In *The Second Battle of Moytura* (*Cath Maige Tured*), it is close to All Hallow's or Samhain when the Dagda—who is the High King of the Tuatha Dé Danann—meets up with the Mórrígan at an appointed place they arranged a year and a day earlier. Her hair is wild and she is standing over a river with one foot on one bank and one foot on the other. The two of them speak and then unite as lovers, and the place where they were was henceforth called "The Bed of the Couple." Afterwards, the Mórrígan tells the Dagda details of the battle to come between his Tuatha De and the Fomorians, whom she pledges to fight against. In this way, she gives both prophecy and Sovereignty, for in mating with the Dagda, she has empowered the leader of the warring faction she has favored to win (Gray, 1983). We will discuss the Mórrígan in more detail later on in this chapter, and it is important to keep the mirror roles of Modron and the Mórrígan in mind.

The essence of Modron's own divinity is preserved in this tale in several ways. Her Otherworldly connections support the reverse euhemerism of divinities that is common in Celtic mythos. Her association with the river is a symbolic call-back to her continental reflex Matrona, who is a river Goddess and divine personification of the river Marne in France. Modron is best known as the mother of Mabon, the Divine Youth or Divine Son, and it is thought that Owain and Morfudd are his half-siblings by a different father. On the other hand, it is intriguing to consider that a potential etymological root for the name Owain is the Welsh word *eoghunn,* which means "youth." Further, Morfudd's name is potentially derived from the Welsh *morwyn,* which means "maiden." Finally, Modron is mentioned in the poem *Cad Goddeu*, "The Battle of the Trees" from *Llyfr Taliesin,* and in it she is paired with someone named Euron. Koch posits that this is a scribal error, and that the redactor meant to write "Gwron", which itself is derived from *Uironos*, which means "divine man, husband, hero"—a possible etymological root for Urien (Koch, 2006). Perhaps, then, Owain is a reflex of Mabon instead of being his half-brother, and the rest of his kin represent a primal and sacred family group: Divine Mother is married to the Divine Man, and she gives birth to the Youth and the Maiden. If such a Divine Family did once exist, their mythos—like that of Matrona and Maponus—has been lost to us.

An intriguing point of information: the archaeological record in the areas along and to the north-west of Hadrian's Wall is rich with artifactual evidence of a strong devotional cultus to Maponus; this north-western area is believed to be the location of Rheged, the Brythonic kingdom ruled by the historical King Urien and his son Owain, after him. The historic Taliesin, considered the greatest of the Early Welsh poets, was a contemporary of Urien and the king was believed to be his patron. The bard wrote praise-poems in honor of Urien and Owain, and Bromwich suggests that some of the poetry in *Llyfr Taliesin* alludes to the name Mabon being used as a pseudonym for Owain. She also points out that during this time period, both in Ireland and in Wales, the attribution of a divine birth for an important historical personage is common, and that it would only serve to further elevate the status of Urien and Owain for the father to have mated with the local sovereignty Goddess, and for the son to be the semi-divine fruit of that union (Bromwich, 2006).

It is quite possible that the story of Modron does not end here. There are multiple sites, churches, and towns in Wales and Cornwall dedicated to, or named for, a saint (or possibly, multiple saints) whose name is variably given as Madron, Madrun, Maderne, and Materiana. In all cases, these names are linked etymologically to Modron and Matrona, and the sites themselves may once have been places where the cultus of the Goddess Modron was strong.

Hagiographic information about St. Modrun tells us she was the granddaughter of Vortigern (the famous, semi-historical 5th century British king), and that her husband and three children were all also saints; like Modron, she had two sons and a daughter. One of the key elements of her story focuses on her fleeing Wales with her youngest son after the battle that killed Vortigern and her husband, the chieftain Ynyr Gwent, before finally settling in Cornwall. (Vermaat, 1999). Madron Well in Cornwall is especially renowned as healing well for children; its waters also had the property of being cool and refreshing for those who are true, while becoming scalding hot at the touch of a traitor (Dunbar, 1905).

It is said that she and her handmaid St. Annun founded a church, which would later be dedicated to them, based on a directive they both received in separate dreams while on pilgrimage to Ynys Elli (Bardsey Island). (Vermaat, 1999) This is an interesting piece of lore, as Ynys Enlli is a potential real-world location for Ynys Afallon, an island of the Otherworld; both islands have strong associations with apples, with the dead, and are places where religious communities were established. As we have seen, Welsh lore states that Afallach is the king of

Ynys Afallon — and Modron is his daughter. The feast days of St. Modrun are given as April 9 and October 19.

The Mórrígan

The Mórrígan is a threefold Irish Goddess, whose name, like that of Rhiannon, means "Great Queen" and can also be traced back to the Gallo-Brittonic Goddess *Rigantona. The Mórrígan is known primarily as a Goddess associated with battle and prophecy, and as her name suggests, she also embodies the Sovereignty of the land. Like Rhiannon, the Mórrígan chooses her mate of her own accord, and as a Sovereignty Goddess, she has the power to grant and rescind kingship over the land (Beck, 2009).

She is made up of a collective of three sisters, and while there are variations on the Goddesses who comprise the Mórrígan, and their areas of divine influence overlap with each other, the most well-known grouping is made up of Mórrigu ("Great Queen") who is primarily concerned with battle, fate, and magic; Babd ("Battle Crow") who often appears as the Washer at the Ford, and who incites warriors to battle; and Macha ("Of the Plain") who is a granter of Sovereignty, a bringer of fertility, and a fierce warrior deity. Of these, it is Macha who holds the most resonance with Rhiannon, as she too possesses equine characteristics.

The Mórrígan is very strongly associated with crows and ravens, and is known to assume their forms. Rhiannon, too, has black birds associated with her, and while their species is never directly identified, the Adar Rhiannon are renowned for the beauty of their song, such that they can lull the living to sleep and bring the dead back to life. Crows are not exactly known for the sweetness of their song, so there appears to be a departure in attendant symbolism. As carrion birds, crows are often found on battlefields, a further reflection of the Mórrígan's martial aspect; this is another difference from Rhiannon, whose extant mythos does not reflect any connection to war, save for the sending of her birds to soothe the souls of those seven warriors who survived the war with Ireland fought in the Second Branch of *Y Mabinogi.*

Interestingly, although Epona was widely worshiped in the Roman military, and was especially revered by the cavalry, she herself is never depicted with any trappings of war; rather, she is almost universally shown seated serenely on a horse with a very calm and peaceful stance, and the majority of the symbols with which she is depicted underscore her connection to fertility and abundance. It is here, however, that the aspect of Epona as a psychopomp may forge a connection between her and the Mórrígan. We shall discuss the symbolism of the horse in detail in chapter five, but for now it is enough to say that it is a potent symbol of Sovereignty as well as a threshold guardian. The liminal nature of the horse therefore makes it a perfect ally to a Goddess that gathers the souls of the war dead to bring to the Otherworld. Perhaps Epona represents a gently aspected psychopomp; as a reflection of her association with the Matronae, she is a comfort to the dying, while the Mórrígan is an inciter, whipping up a battle fury that embraces war as an honorable death.

Differences aside, it is of great importance to note that unlike Rhiannon and other figures from Welsh legends, the Mórrígan and other prominent figures are specifically identified as divinities in early Irish literature. For example, in *The Metrical Dindshenchas,* which was written down during the 11th century, but which is believed to have existed in oral tradition since at least the 5th or 6th century (Westrop, 1899), we have the following:

ben in Dagda,
ba samla día sóach.
...in Mórrígan mórda,
ba slóg-dírmach sámda.
Metrical Dindshenchas: Odras

the wife of the Dagda
a phantom was the shapeshifting goddess
...the mighty Morrigan
whose ease is trooping hosts
(Translation by Morgan Daimler)

That the Gods are still identified as such in early literary works and are not simply Otherworldly figures is significant; it is likely the result of Ireland, unlike Britain, remaining free of Roman annexation, its attendant early Christianization, and the subsequent societal collapse and waves of invasion that resulted after Roman withdrawal from the British Isles 400 years later. The Irish therefore held on to their Pagan beliefs and social structures longer than the Celts of Britain and the continent, and began to write them down sooner. The happy consequence of this is that of all the Celtic cultures, the Irish possess the largest corpus of myth and lore; and while all of the Celts possessed distinct, yet related cultures, it is possible to look for parallels both in story and with divinities to help fill in some (very strongly-qualified) blanks in the Brythonic traditions, especially when there are also similarities in Gallic cultures.

Macha

Although she is one of the three sisters who make up the tripartite Goddess Mórrígan, a separate consideration of Macha reveals some evocative connections with Rhiannon specifically and perhaps reveals some of the root Indo-European religious constructs surrounding the sacred function of the Horse Goddess in general. There are several stories in Irish lore about Macha, although it is unclear if these are all the same person, or if, indeed, they are all divinities. The most famous story of Macha comes from the *Noinden Ulad (The Debility of the Ulstermen).*

In this tale, Macha is married to an Ulsterman named Crundchu mac Agnomain, and her presence in his life brings him abundance and wealth. She becomes pregnant by him, and though she is close to her term, he tells her that he is going to attend the great assembly of the Ulstermen. She implores him not to go, saying that if he were to speak of her at the assembly, their union would be ended. He promises to keep silent about her, and leaves to attend the festival. He is unable to keep his word, however, and boasts to all assembled that his wife could run faster than the king's pair of champion horses.

The king has Crundchu imprisoned, and sends his men to bring Macha to the assembly to prove her husband's boast by racing his horses. She asks for a delay because she is about to give birth, but the king refuses and threatens to kill Crundchu on the spot if she will not race. Macha appeals to the crowd for their help, but her plea for mercy is once more rejected, so she tells the king to bring up his horses, and the race begins. She easily outruns them both, and with a cry of pain, gives birth to twins at the finish line before the horses even arrive. The place of the assembly was from then on called Emain Macha—the Twins of Macha. Those who heard her cry of pain themselves became overcome with the pains of a birthing woman and so she lays her curse on them:

> From this hour the ignominy that you have inflicted upon me will redound to the shame of each one of you. When a time of oppression falls upon you, each one of you who dwells in this province will be overcome with weakness, as the weakness of a woman in childbirth, and this will remain upon you for five days and four nights; to the ninth generation it shall be so. (Hull, 1989, pg. 100)

This curse has terrible repercussions during the *Táin Bó Cuailnge* (*Cattle Raid of Cooley*), as it delays the Ulstermen from entering the battle.

The king in this tale of Macha is the famous Conchobar,

who was so highly regarded by his people that he was given the *droit du seigneur* to sleep with a bride before her wedding night and also to have the right to sleep with the wife of whoever was providing hospitality to him. On one such occasion, he demanded this right from a woman named Dechtire, whom he did not recognize as his sister at the time; she too asked for a delay as she was in labor—which Conchobar granted. Dechtire nevertheless gave birth to a child that looked like Conchobar—a child who would grow to be the great hero Cú Chulainn. At the moment of his birth, a mare in the household gave birth to two foals, and these were gifted to the boy; they would later pull his chariot in battle, and one of them was called Liath Macha, or "Grey of Macha" (Hull, 1989).

There are several parallels between the stories of Macha and Rhiannon. Both are forced to take on the role of a horse; Macha, by racing horses, and Rhiannon by offering to carry visitors on her back from where she sat on a mounting block. Both of them give birth to twins of a sort. Rhiannon doesn't directly do so; her giving birth to Pryderi is paired with the foaling of Teyrnon's white mare which is, in many ways, her avatar. Both Irish and Welsh myth feature the gifting of the horse born at the same time as them to a hero, and even though Cú Chulainn is not the child of Macha, that one of his "twinned" horses nevertheless bears her name is worthy of note.

Dexter believes that the twinning is an important element of these tales, as they harken back to the Indo-European mythos of the divine twins, sometimes manifesting as a divine horseman and his brother, or as twin horsemen, or else as a human and a horse birthed together from the same mother, who is most certainly a Goddess. She also posits that the mytheme of a hippomorphic Goddess who is punished after childbirth is really a memory of the Indo-European horse sacrifice. This rite was not undertaken lightly; horses were too valuable and of high status to be sacrificed with any regularity. Instead, the intention of the ritual was to renew the power of the kingship, and most often included sexual congress between the king and a mare, although some Indian iterations involved the queen and a stallion (Dexter, 1990).

Gerald Cambrensis, also known as Gerald of Wales, relates an Irish version of this horse sacrifice in his 1187 work *Topographia Hiberniae,* which is significant not only because this was a kingship ritual granting Sovereignty, but because it also takes place in Ulster—whose royal seat is none other than Emain Macha:

> When the whole people of that land has been gathered together in one place, a white mare is brought forward into the middle of the assembly. He who is to be inaugurated, not as a chief, but as an outlaw, has bestial intercourse with her before all, professing himself to be a beast also. The mare is then killed immediately, cut up in pieces, and boiled in water. A bath is prepared for the man afterwards in the same water. He sits in the bath surrounded by all his people, and all, he and they, eat of the meat of the mare which is brought to them. He quaffs and drinks of the broth in which he is bathed, not in any cup, or using his hand, but just dipping his mouth into it round about him. When this unrighteous rite has been carried out, his kingship and dominion have been conferred. (O'Meara 1951, 1982, p. 109 – 110)

Dexter believes that the mythological memory of this act is present wherever there are Horse Goddesses, especially when their fecundity is signaled by the birthing of twins. Because these are Goddesses, they cannot die as a sacrificed animal would, and so they are shown mythically to undergo a punishment instead (Dexter, 1990). We will look further at the symbolism of the horse in chapter five.

International Folk Motifs

If we look at the story of Rhiannon from a purely literary perspective, we find that she serves as a clear example of several international folk motifs, a fact that may be of some consequence when it comes to determining the status of her potential or former divinity. An international folk motif is a narrative element that can be found both across stories and across cultures. These are identifiable patterns which appear in international popular tales that may not have any direct relationship to each other, but which nonetheless employ similar identifiable plot devices. The Stith Thompson *Motif-Index of Folk-Literature* is a six-volume collection of these motifs, originally gathered primarily from European stories, which have been classified and cataloged numerically using the Aarne-Thompson tale type index. This, and its modern expansions, is an invaluable tool for the study of folklore and mythology, and it is especially useful for comparative literary analysis.

Although the entirety of the First and Third Branches, and indeed the whole of *Y Mabinogi*, feature many folk motifs, there are three which apply specifically to Rhiannon and her story. On the outset, she represents a variant of the Fairy Bride motif, which has very specific manifestations in Wales especially (Wood, 1992); she is an Otherworldly maiden who falls in love with and marries a mortal. She does not quite fit into his world, however, and through careless action, he loses her and she returns to the Otherworld. In Rhiannon's case, Pwyll loses her more than once. The first time is when he promises Gwawl anything he desires, and Gwawl asks for Rhiannon's hand; she must remain in the Otherworld for a year without Pwyll until she can set a new feast and Pwyll can convince Gwawl to give her up again. The second time is after the disappearance of their newborn son, which sets the stage for the next motif—that of the Calumniated Wife.

The Calumniated or Falsely Accused Wife is a very well-attested international folk motif, with many sub-motifs, several of which are present in Rhiannon's story. She is an innocent woman who has been accused of killing her newborn child—worse, the First Branch infers that she is accused of having devoured the child, and puppy bones are planted as evidence of what she has done (Jackson, 1961). That these story elements appear in other tales as well is somewhat shocking, but Hemming believes that while Rhiannon's tale is very likely to have been influenced by other tales with the same motifs, it on its own cannot fully explain her story, especially taking the horse elements into account (Hemming, 1998).

Lastly, we have the motif of Sovereignty personified, which is a prominent motif in Celtic legend that takes many forms over the course of the literary traditions of Ireland, Wales, and Brittany. In the case of the Four Branches, this motif is symbolic and subtextual, and is something we will be examining at length in chapter five.

When we consider the existence of international folk motifs, we need to ask why it is that popular tales—tales which likely have their origins in oral tradition—feature narrative elements that can be found in different cultures separated both in space and in time. There are several explanations for why this might be so. The first takes into account the origins of the motif, and posits that 1) either the motif in question reflects a human experience so common across cultures that the motif is *polygenic*, that is, it arose independently in different areas, or 2) the motif originally arose as part of the story tradition of an ancestral culture, and as people and ideas migrated to different places, they took the stories with them; these stories then evolved to reflect the changes in culture over time, but still held on to some of the core narrative elements.

In addition to origin, we must also consider that the method of a tale's diffusion will also impact the story. In the case of horizontal transmission, neighboring areas and cultures influence each other, sharing stories and infusing them with details and narrative shifts that ripple outward and come to reflect local cultural relevance. Vertical transmission, on the other hand, sees one generation passing its stories down to the next generation, and the changes in the tale reflect the shifts in the social, political, and cultural landscapes within which it comes to dwell as it descends down the lineage of tradition. These can both happen simultaneously and therefore may be one way to account for the spread of international folk motifs.

The Big Picture

These considerations around transmission may be what we can use to ultimately account for Rhiannon's subtextual divinity— whether from a literary or mythological perspective. She is clearly connected to the Goddess Epona, who is believed to be a specialized reflex of Matrona—a Gallo-Roman Divine Mother Goddess who may be a singular iteration of the typically triform Dea Matronae, believed to be of Continental Celtic origin. Matrona has a Welsh cognate in Modron, the Divine Mother whose Divine Son Mabon is a cognate of Matrona's son Maponus. This mother/ son dyad is considered to be the template for the story of Rhiannon and Pryderi, as they both share in the mytheme of the stolen and imprisoned child. Another potential pathway of connection exists when we look at Rhiannon's connection to *Rigantona. There is of course an etymological link, as their names both mean "Divine Queen", a fact which also connects them to the Irish Mórrígan, who is directly attested to be divine in Irish mythos. It may also be of note that one of Epona's Roman appellations is Epona Regina, meaning "Divine Horse Queen", underscoring her connection to Sovereignty (Hemming, 1998).

With all of these considerations we can comfortably say that Rhiannon is a Goddess, although her divinity is subsumed from an earlier form than that which was eventually set into writing during the medieval period in Wales. While shifts in culture, evolution of language, and influences from foreign lands shaped the Divine Queen of the Celtic Britons into the being that we know as Rhiannon, the fierceness of her spirit, the enormity of her heart, and the strength of her noble bearing persist. No matter what name we call her, no matter how much of her story we have remembered or have forgotten she is the Divine Mother, the Sovereign Mare, and the Great Queen. And she has much yet to teach us.

Chapter Five

Aspects of the Divine Queen

Now that we have recounted her stories and established the potential lineage of her divinity, let us look to the mythic and cultural roles played by Rhiannon, and examine the areas of her concern.

Lady of the Otherworld

Rhiannon has strong associations with the Otherworld, both directly through her person, and indirectly through the animals, items, and events connected with her. When we first see her in the First Branch, she rides out from the Gorsedd Arberth—a wondrous mound that promises to any noble who sits upon it either that they will be witness to a wonder, or else receive many wounds and blows. In Celtic lore, mounds and fairy hills are considered liminal places which serve as portals to the Otherworld, and are often portrayed in legend as places where the Fair Folk would come to feast, or where humans could pass through into the Otherworld for what they thought was a night, only to return to find that a hundred years had passed, or where someone could dare to sleep under the hill with the fate of either returning with the poetic gift or else becoming consumed by madness.

These beliefs may perhaps be a reflection of the Neolithic indigenous British practice of burying their dead in artificial earthworks, such as megalithic long barrows and single-chambered dolmen tombs which were covered with earth to form hill-shaped tumuli. It was to these burial places that the ancient Britons would bring offerings of food to their beloved dead, and it is possible that they practiced a form of ancestor worship. It is a testimony to their belief in an afterlife that many of these burial mounds had seasonal solar (and occasionally lunar) alignments, where on certain astronomically significant days, such as the Winter Solstice, a beam of light would enter the dark earthen chamber to illuminate a carving on the back wall or central upright stone, or else serve as a visual metaphor of the revitalizing energies of the sun piercing the darkness of the tomb to symbolically implant new life.

It's difficult to say with any certainty that there is a direct connection, but it is possible that the folkloric associations of hills and mounds with the Otherworld remained even after the names and cultures of those who may have been interred within them had fallen away. Perhaps a vague sense of the original function and purpose of these mounds may have lingered to inform the belief that transformed these ancestral burials into magical portals into the Otherworld; indeed, there appears to be a hint of cultural memory which underscores the folk beliefs around fairy mounds, some of which persist into the present day. It is likely, then, that the contemporary medieval audience would have understood the significance of this magical hill, and would immediately have seen Rhiannon's emergence from the mound as a clear proclamation of her Otherworldly origins. Even if this were not the case, there are other signs that Rhiannon is no ordinary human woman, and they are immediately apparent.

When we first meet her, Rhiannon is described as, "wearing a shining golden garment of brocaded silk" (Davies, 2007, pg. 8). Earlier in the First Branch, the exact same description is given to the clothing that Pwyll is dressed in when he takes on the likeness of Arawn, king of Annwn; Arawn's unnamed wife and Queen is also garbed in this fashion. When Gwawl, Rhiannon's rejected suitor, comes to the wedding feast of Rhiannon and Pwyll, he too is dressed in silk brocade. Later on in the story, Rhiannon's infant son is found swaddled in a mantle of brocaded silk. Very few characters are described in the First Branch as wearing what, in the middle ages, would have been an incredibly expensive and high status fabric, and while this detail may have been included in the story to simply mark the noble stature of these figures, that the garb appears to have been reserved only for those characters who are associated with Annwn is potentially significant, and may serve as another marker for the Otherworld.

Another potent characteristic of the Otherworld is that where its influence is present, the normal rules governing the passage of time and the measure of space do not apply; the unchanging and unhurried gait of Rhiannon's white horse, which nevertheless could not be overtaken no matter how long or how hard another rider pursued her, is a clear example of this kind of distortion and is probably the defining experience of our introduction to her. It is likely that the magical speed of her horse, or perhaps its ability to warp the passage of time in a way that prevented anyone from catching up with them, would have marked Rhiannon as an Otherworldly figure to the contemporary medieval audience. This phenomenon is also present in the Second Branch where the British survivors of a terrible war in Ireland spend almost 80 years feasting in a grand hall on what appears to be an Otherworldly island, where they never aged, and dwelt with joy and without memory for the tragedies they had endured—even feasting and communing with the head of their dead king.

In addition to the Otherworld's ability to distort time, it also had a tendency to disregard the limitations of distance and volume with its magic. Later in the First Branch, Rhiannon gives Pwyll a small bag that would never run out of room no matter how much food was placed in it until a wealthy and landed nobleman trampled down the food with both feet, and declared, "Enough has been put in here" (Davies 2007, pg. 14). And again, in the Second Branch, the Adar Rhiannon appear to the feasting war survivors, and sing to them a song so beautiful that every other song in the world was unlovely in comparison. The birds appeared to be across the water and very far away from the island, but simultaneously, they felt and sounded as if they were in the feasting hall with the men.

Perhaps related to the Otherworld's ability to warp physical limitations, or else as a byproduct of the reverse euhemerization process examined earlier, Rhiannon is depicted as having superhuman strength when she accepts Pwyll's unjust and perhaps bizarre judgment that she be punished for the destruction of their infant son; she was required to sit on a horse block outside of Arberth for seven years, telling all comers the story of her alleged crime, and offering to carry them into the court on her back. While the First Branch is quick to say that very few visitors accepted her offer, the subtext is that some did and no mention is made of her inability to do so. Further, Rhiannon's nurses concocted an apparently believable story that their queen, who had just given birth, was able to fight all seven of them off as they tried to prevent her from destroying her son, and finally, in the Third Branch, Rhiannon is said to have carried asses' collars on her shoulders as she labored in the Otherworld. This is no fragile human woman, clearly, and her strength seems to mirror the larger than life appearance of Bendigeidfran in the Second Branch; indeed, the king of the Island of the Mighty was described as a giant for whom no house was ever built that could contain him.

Goddess of Sovereignty

The quest for Sovereignty is a well-known international folk motif which is an important element in many tales from Ireland and Wales, and which also plays an important thematic role in Arthurian legends. This popular narrative theme features a candidate for kingship entering into a *hieros gamos*, or sacred marriage, with a representative of the land. Sometimes the Sovereignty was embodied by a tutelary Goddess who appeared to the would-be-king in the form of a woman, while other traditions utilized symbolic or totemic representations of Sovereignty as seen with the mating of Irish kings with a white mare, which was later sacrificed and eaten.

The Sovereignty figure is quite overt in Irish lore, often appearing as a hideous hag who tests potential kings; when they mate, she is transformed into a beautiful maiden, and the land is likewise transformed by the energies of the new king. In Welsh mythos, the figure of Sovereignty shifts to be more subtextual, while in later Arthurian legend the quest for Sovereignty becomes purely symbolic in some tales—as with the quest for the cauldron or grail— and in other stories, shifts from a Goddess granting a king rulership over the land, to a man in authority granting a woman sovereignty over herself.

Seeming to bridge these two manifestations of tradition—the direct identification of Sovereignty in Irish lore and the indirect symbolism of the cauldron or grail quests in Arthurian legends— the Welsh materials require that we rely upon an analysis of subtext to find the representations of Sovereignty in the Four Branches and their associated tales; it is worth wondering if these thematic undercurrents would have been obvious to the medieval Welsh audience of these stories.

There are several archetypal parameters defining the personification and function of Sovereignty:

1. She is a representative of the land, often a tutelary deity or spirit.
2. She is encountered at liminal places and times—such as bodies of water, land boundaries, areas associated with the Otherworld, dusk and dawn, holy days.
3. She presents challenges to the would-be king, determining his worth and initiating sexual contact.
4. She enters into a *hieros gamos,* or sacred marriage, with a kingly candidate, sealing the fortunes of the land to the health and actions of the man she has, through this act, made king.
5. She has the power to grant, and rescind if circumstances require, sovereignty over the land.

6. She has the ability to change shape, often as a reflection of the status of the land in relationship to the righteous king.

Let us briefly examine these points as they concern Rhiannon's marriages.

Rhiannon and Pwyll – Sovereignty in the First Branch.

1. Rhiannon is not directly stated to be a representative of the land, although she is coded with Otherworldly associations through her magical white horse, her fine garb, her greater-than-human strength, and magical objects like the bag she gives to Pwyll.
2. She rides out from the Otherworld on a white horse, itself a symbol of Sovereignty and a threshold guardian, and she is associated with a magical mound.
3. Rhiannon tests Pwyll by remaining out of his reach as they ride until he asks for her to stop. Pwyll's loss of Rhiannon to her former suitor, and then (with her assistance) clever retrieval of her a year later is also a test—one he passes—as he defeats his rival and frees Rhiannon of the obligation to wed him. Pwyll's worth was initially tested by the powers of the Otherworld when he faced off Arawn's enemy at an Annuvian ford, possibly a re-enactment of the seasonal sovereignty motif of one king overcoming the other, and being chosen by Sovereignty to rule over the next season or seasonal cycle.
4. Pwyll finally weds Rhiannon in her father's Otherworldly court, before they return to his own land. While Pwyll was already a Pendefig Dyfed (a prince), and obtained a second name Pen Annwn after his year in Annwn, it is possible that his marriage to Rhiannon granted him true authority over his lands.
5. Rhiannon rejects Gwawl, and choses to marry Pwyll

instead—an act that could be seen as Sovereignty choosing her mate based on his worthiness. She also gifts Pwyll with a magical bag that cannot be filled in order to assist him in defeating Gwawl. This bag is a possible symbolic reflex of a womb in the same way a cauldron can be, therefore representing the underlying sexual nature of the granting of Sovereignty.

6. When Rhiannon is unpartnered or in a position of imbalance with her partner, she is seen either riding a horse, or taking on an equine aspect by inviting others to ride her like a horse. She is also seen as a double of Teyrnon's magnificent white mare, as both of them give birth on the same day, and both lose their offspring almost immediately after birth.

Rhiannon's first husband was Pywll, whose name means "discretion", "good sense", or "wisdom" (McKenna, 1980). He was Pendefig Dyfed, the prince of Dyfed, a kingdom in South Wales. The First Branch of *Y Mabinogi* is named for him, and the first act of the tale demonstrates what could only be considered an enormous *lack* of "good sense" on his part. While out hunting with his dogs one day, Pwyll comes upon a stag that had been felled by a pack of white dogs with red ears; he calls those dogs off and sets his own animals to feast upon the deer. Unfortunately for him, the strange dogs belong to Arawn, the king of Annwn, and Pwyll's actions cause great insult to the Otherworldly king, who soon arrives in search of his dogs.

After realizing he was in the wrong because, as a crowned king, Arawn outranked him and therefore had greater claim to the deer, Pwyll sought to make amends with him. The two agree upon an arrangement whereby they would switch places with each other for a year with each taking on the visage of the other and ruling their respective kingdoms in their stead. At the end of the year, Pwyll—still in the guise of Arawn—would go to a ford in Annwn where he would engage an enemy of Arawn in one-on-one battle. Arawn and Hafgan, a neighboring Annuvian king, had battled each other annually in this place, with one never able to get the better of the other. Arawn instructs Pwyll to strike only one blow with his sword, no matter how Hafgan would plead to be finished off by another; it is only through dealing the singular blow that Hafgan could be defeated.

The details of the battle evoke the ancient motif of the eternal struggle between the light and the dark, or between summer and winter. Arawn, whose name is thought to mean "He of the Sown Field" forever battles Hafgan, whose name means "Summer Light" or "Summer Song", the king of the lands adjacent to his in Annwn. The battle taking place at a river ford is significant as it is one of those magical liminal places we see so often in Celtic myth—places that are boundaries between the worlds. Too, when we see Pwyll exchange places with the Lord of Annwn, the two meet at a boundary between the two lands, and share a wife, although Pwyll chooses not to consummate with her. It may be that these elements are remnants of sovereignty rites where the Lord of the Winter supplants the Lord of the Summer, only to give way again in six months' time—each taking turns as mate to the Goddess of the Land.

It is also possible that Pwyll's keeping chaste with Arawn's wife may have been a test. Described in the text as an exquisitely beautiful woman next to whom Pwyll slept for the entirety of a year—a woman who believed that Pwyll was in fact Arawn, her husband—he nevertheless did not engage with her sexually, even after Arawn had explicitly told Pwyll he could lie with her. This loyalty surprised Arawn greatly and further endeared the Prince of Dyfed to him. This test of purity is mirrored in the late 14th-century tale, *Sir Gawain and the Green Knight*, which also contains a coded Sovereignty figure.

Although the narrative is fairly clear that Pryderi's father is Pwyll, in a mythic context he has more than one father—all of whom appear to have complex and symbolically overlapping relationships with Rhiannon. Ostensibly a mortal prince at the onset, Pwyll's relationship with Arawn and his victory over Hafgan in the Otherworld shifted his domain somewhat, rendering him a Lord of Annwn—Pwyll Pen Annwn. It is after he receives this name and forges an alliance with Arawn that Rhiannon rides forth from the Otherworld, seeking to marry him. The strong connection that Pwyll has with the Otherworld appears to underscore this union; even their marriage takes place in an Otherworldly realm, at the court of Rhiannon's father.

Stolen from Rhiannon on the night he was born, the infant Pryderi was inexplicably found, swaddled in golden brocade, on the threshold of the house of Teyrnon Twryf Liant, a nobleman who was a vassal of Pwyll. Teyrnon possessed a beautiful mare who gave birth every May Eve, and whose foal always disappeared that very night. It is not difficult to see the parallels between Teyrnon's horses and the circumstances of Pryderi's birth, and there are several other connections of note.

Rhiannon and Teyrnon's horse are essentially doubles for each other. They both give birth and lose their offspring on the same day—and it is May Eve, a portal day that blurs the boundaries between this world and the Otherworld. Although the horse has apparently lost several foals in the past, it is on this particular night that Teyrnon keeps vigil, and because of this, he is able to rescue both the newborn horse and the infant Pryderi—who is discovered in yet another liminal place: the threshold of the house. Teyrnon brings the child to his unnamed wife, and together they decide to raise the boy as their own. The child grew preternaturally quickly, reaching a height and displaying a skill level of children twice his age. He possessed an incredible affinity for horses, and when he reached four years of age, although appearing and acting much older, Teyrnon's wife suggested that the boy be given the colt that had been born on the same night as he; in effect, the boy and the colt are mirrors of each other as well.

On the surface, the fosterage by Teyrnon of Rhiannon's missing son seems fairly straightforward. It was a common practice for members of nobility to foster their children in other courts as a way to forge bonds of friendship, to shore up alliances, and to share wealth between them. Aside from the supernatural intervention that brought the boy that he named Gwri Wallt Euryn ("Blooming Golden Hair") to his literal doorstep, this fosterage would have resonated as a cultural expectation for the contemporary Welsh audience. However, when we look a little deeper, there appears to be something else going on here, the explanation for which scholars have sought to resolve for a very long time (Koch, 2006).

To begin with, Teryrnon's very name is intriguing. Featuring the terminal deific "-on", which we've already seen in the names of Rhiannon, Modron, and Mabon, we are immediately alerted to the idea that Teyrnon is not an ordinary supporting character (Hamp, 1999). Ford gives Teyrnon Twryf Liant's full name to mean "Lord of the Tempestuous Sea" (Ford, 1982) His first name appears to be the Middle Welsh form of the Celtic name *Tigernonos, meaning "Divine or Great Lord"—a direct mirror of Rhiannon's "Divine or Great Queen" derivation from "*Rigantona" (Davies, 2006). While we have no direct proof of the existence of *Rigantona and *Tigernonos as early Celtic deities aside from their reconstructed names, it is difficult to consider it purely a coincidence that the names of Pryderi's birth mother and foster father are such perfect reflections of each other. This is what led influential early Celticists, Sir Edward Anwyl and William John Gruffydd, to posit that Teyrnon, and not Pwyll, was Pryderi's father (Hutton, 2011). Gruffydd further developed the theory that the story of Pryderi's birth and childhood as depicted in the First Branch is a very garbled version of the original story which the medieval redactor struggled to reconstruct using fragments of the tale, which Gruffydd believed ultimately had its source in Irish mythos (Gruffydd, 1953).

While Gruffydd's ideas are fascinating, and the various pieces of information that he weaves together are worthy of study by scholars and Brythonic Pagans alike, current scholarship discounts most of his conclusions, in large part due to lack of supporting evidence. Modern scholar Patrick K. Ford finds it difficult to believe that the redactor of *Y Mabinogi* was writing down something they didn't understand; given the amount of time involved as well as the expense of the vellum used, Ford feels that what was retained — and the form in which it was preserved — was intentional and purposeful (Ford, 1981/1982).

Rhiannon and Manawydan – Sovereignty in the Third Branch.

1. Although Rhiannon is not directly stated to be a representative of the land, Pryderi offers his friend, Manawydan, rulership over the seven cantrefs he inherited from his father Pwyll as well as the hand of Rhiannon in marriage; the linking of the two may subtextually signify Rhiannon's role as a tutelary Goddess of Dyfed.

2. Manawydan's first encounter with Rhiannon was without a doubt, solidly Otherworldly. Both he and Pryderi were two of the seven survivors of the war in Ireland that was fought in the Second Branch, and they both experienced the Adar Rhiannon — the Otherworldly Birds of Rhiannon — sing for them while they were feasting at Harlech.

3. While perhaps not directly challenging Manawydan to test his worthiness, the now-widowed Rhiannon does meet with him at her son's suggestion, and apparently finds him worthy to be her mate as she chooses to marry him that very day.

4. Rhiannon and Manawydan sleep together after feasting, and he takes over administration and enjoyment of the

seven cantrefs of Dyfed.

5. Pryderi maintains legal lordship, however, and travels to the court of Caswallon to give homage to the British king. When he returns, and sits upon the Gorsedd Arberth with his mother, wife, and Manawydan, the Otherworld intervenes and all of Dyfed is divested of people, human habitation, and domesticated animals. The land has reverted to a wild state, and has become a Wasteland of sorts. This may relate to the imbalance of rule both in Dyfed and in Britain as a whole: the ruler of Dyfed has given power to another, and the one who should be king of the Island of the Mighty has not taken up his throne. The Wasteland theme in later grail mythos is a reflection of the lame or wounded king, and something similar may be happening in Dyfed subtextually.

6. Manawydan's inaction around rescuing Pryderi caused his relationship with Sovereignty to be negatively impacted, and coupled with his failure to assert his right to the throne he may not have been considered the right candidate for the role he had undertaken. Manawydan earns the right to rule by correctly, and ethically, restoring Dyfed to its abundant form; in the end, his wisdom and patience wins the day in contrast to Pryderi's impetuous nature. When Rhiannon and Pryderi are restored to Dyfed, along with the people and animals that were previously gone, we see that Rhiannon had once again "shapechanged" while out of right relationship with her husband: she was required to wear asses' collars after bailing hay. Rhiannon returns to him, no longer laboring like a work horse in the Otherworld.

Rhiannon's second husband is Manawydan fab Llŷr, the son of the Sea, who is brother to Bran and Branwen. We know very little about Llŷr, who is himself the son of the solar deity Beli Mawr, although the etymology of his name suggests that he was once a Brythonic sea deity. Although Manawydan's name is almost directly cognate to Manannán mac Lir, the Irish Sea God who dwells upon the namesake Island of Man, there is very little else that directly ties him to Manannán. There is nothing of the ocean about Manawydan, who is instead a master craftsman, an agriculturalist, and one who embodies critical thinking and strategies, rather than the fire of a warrior. Named as one of the Three Golden Shoemakers in the Trioedd Ynys Prydein, some believe that his name derives from the Brythonic word for awl, a shoemaker's tool.

There is, however, a strong connection between water, or water divinities, and horses in many Indo-European cultures; Poseidon created the horse in Greek mythology, for example. In Celtic traditions, there are several connections between horses and the sea: Macha is the daughter Sainreth mac Imbaith, "Nature of the Sea" (Ford, 1977); Manannán mac Lir's chariot is pulled across the waves by Enbarr, a horse with a flowing mane; after the death of Cú Chulainn, Liath Macha, one of the twin horses born at the same time as the hero, returns to the water; and in Welsh lore, Teyrnon Twryf Liant, a horse lord and another potential mate to Rhiannon, is also associated with water as suggested by the meaning of his name: "Lord of the Tempestuous Sea." Perhaps the association between water and horses has something to do with their shared property of liminality. We will discuss this aspect of the horse further later on in this chapter and we've already seen several examples of the ways in which bodies of water, especially rivers and fords, are considered threshold places where this world meets the Otherworld. It is probably not coincidental that one of Manannán's functions as a Sea God is to guard the gateway to the Otherworld. Indeed, in Irish mythology especially, one must undertake an Immrama, or journey across the water, in order to reach the Islands of the Otherworld.

While Rhiannon does not figure as prominently in the Third

Branch as she does in the First, her subtextual identity as a Sovereignty Goddess is clearly present, albeit tempered by the filter of contemporary medieval Welsh society. The story of the Third Branch is a direct continuation of the events of the Second Branch, wherein the great war in Ireland saw only seven of the British warriors dispatched to Ireland survive the war; Pryderi, son of Rhiannon and Pwyll, and Manawydan among them.

When the two men, who are fast friends, return to Britain, they retreat to Dyfed where Pryderi offers both the hand of his now-widowed mother and rulership over his seven cantrifs to Manawydan. This demonstrates a key point of inheritance law: Rhiannon does not gain ownership of her husband's land after his death; it passes down through him to her son. However, Rhiannon is shown to have some say in the matter of her remarriage:

> Then Manawydan and Rhiannon sat together and began to converse; and as a result of that conversation, his head and heart grew tender towards her, and he was delighted that he had never seen a woman who as fairer or more beautiful than her.
> 'Pryderi,' he said, 'I will agree to your proposal.'
> 'What was that?' said Rhiannon.
> 'My lady,' said Pryderi, 'I have given you as a wife to Manawydan son of Llŷr.'
> 'I will agree to that gladly,' said Rhiannon.
> 'I am glad too,' said Manawydan, 'and may God repay the man who gives me such firm friendship.' Before that feast finished, he slept with her. (Davies 2007, p. 36)

While it may seem odd that Pryderi would act as a matchmaker for his mother, this is consistent with medieval Welsh convention, and illustrates the standing of women in medieval Wales. A woman is under the legal authority and protection of the men in her life: when she is single, she is under the authority of her father or brothers; when married, she is under the guardianship of her husband; and when widowed, she is either under her son's protection, or the responsibility for her reverts back to her kin group if she is without sons (Valente, 1986). However, this authority has some limits, and the Welsh Laws of Women are explicit in stating that women cannot be given in marriage against their will (Van der Linden, 2007).

All of this is illustrated clearly in the exchanges between Pryderi, Manawydan, and Rhiannon. It is the gifting of lordship over the seven cantrifs of Dyfed that stands out as an oddity here, and its apparent bundling with the offer of marriage to Rhiannon may suggest that rulership over these lands is a consequence of receiving the blessing of the tutelary spirit of the land — by entering into a sacred marriage with the local sovereignty Goddess who is, in this case, Rhiannon. It is noteworthy that as Bran's brother, and in the absence of an heir in Bran's lineage, Manawydan should have assumed the throne of Britain. That he did not contest the kingship of Caswallon because he did not want to start yet another war is a testimony to the measured wisdom of Manawydan, which is a feature in the events of the Third Branch; because of this, he is remembered as one of the Three Undemanding Chieftains in a Welsh Triad.

The Great Horsewoman

Rhiannon's association with horses in the narrative of the Four Branches is well attested; it is deliberate, symbolic, and repetitive. When she arrives in the First Branch we see her astride a magical white horse that, even when walking, could be overtaken by no other horse. Later, when her newborn son is spirited away by a monster, the child is found on the threshold of a stall with a mare whose own foals disappear annually on the first of May, a significant and liminal feast day marking the beginning of summer.

Falsely accused of having destroyed the missing baby,

Rhiannon is sentenced by Pwyll, her husband, to a bizarre punishment involving her sitting on a mounting block outside of the castle for seven years. While there, she must recount the details of her alleged crime to strangers and offer to bear them on her back into the court. In the Third Branch, when she is imprisoned in an Otherworldly fortress with her son Pryderi, she is made to wear the collars of asses after they had been out been hauling hay. The repetitive horse imagery is significant in that it ties Rhiannon to the equine Sovereignty Goddess with whom the king must mate to legitimize his kingship both in Celtic and in other Indo-European traditions. "The worship of and connection between the horse and the fertility goddess, known among the continental Celts as Epona, has been documented as common practice in Europe" (McKenna, 1980, p. 317).

The symbol of the horse ties into the Trifunctional Theory of influential mythologist Georges Dumézil. He posited that Proto-Indo-European culture was made up of three groups, which in turn, performed three separate social functions: Sovereignty, consisting of kings, judges, and priests; Military, concerned with war and protection; and Fertility, which was connected to food production, craftsmanship, and general prosperity. In this schema, the horse symbolizes the first function, although it relied greatly on the other two functions to be effective. This is why the Horse Goddess is often considered a transfunctional figure (Lyle, 1982).

The significance of the horse has a long history in Wales, dating back to pre-Christian times. As we have seen, horse divinities such as the Gaulish Epona, the Irish Macha, and the Welsh Rhiannon are prominent in Celtic culture, and these goddesses appear to be concerned with healing, fertility, and death. The horse also figured markedly in a Romano-Celtic divine horseman cult, where these divinities seem to have played roles both as protectors and healers (Green, 1997).

Furthermore, there are what appear to be sacrificial burials of horses evidenced all over the Celtic world. The association of these cult deposits with locations which had liminal qualities — that is, which straddled two different worlds, such as land boundaries or areas marking the transition between sacred and profane space — may indicate that the horse was thought of as dwelling in both worlds, perhaps because they were part wild and part domestic. This seems to be consistent with the later Welsh custom of burying the heads of horses under the thresholds of houses, under hearths, or straddling the chimney in order to prevent evil spirits from entering the home (Green, 1997). This connection with the liminality of threshold places further underscores the horse's association with sovereignty since Sovereignty figures themselves are bridges between states of being.

The Welsh folk practice of the Mari Lwyd ("Grey Mare") may also be a reflection of the liminal quality of the horse. Although it is tempting to see this winter tradition as a remnant of ancient Pagan practice, we only have proof of it dating back to the 18th century. The Mari Lwyd is thought to have been a wassailing tradition, which was a ritual of communal drinking believed to impart abundance, increased fertility, and good fortune to all who partook of the drink. In the Mari Lwyd tradition, a man wearing a horse costume fashioned from the skull of a horse traveled with a retinue which visited homes and public houses, and sought entrance to each by engaging in an *ex tempore* battle of verses with those within; if the Mari party won, they were let inside to join a feast (Owen, 1985). While this may have been an example of sympathetic magic, which brought fertility and abundance to the household, the Mari Lwyd also served a practical purpose: bringing communities together during the more isolated winter months, and sharing food with neighbors at a time when, especially in rural areas, it had become scarcer.

It is significant, however, that the practice was tied into the liminal qualities of the season, the transitional time between the old year and the new — between the barrenness of late winter at Christmas, and the first signs of spring celebrated at Candlemas. One can see this as a reflection of the desire of the Mari Lwyd party to want to cross over the more literal threshold into the home (Wood, 1997). This echoes the Celtic conception of the horse as guardian and psychopomp, and its presence at this interstitial time assists in bridging this world and the Otherworld, in order to allow new and fertile energies to replace the fallowness of the dying year. Some modern Pagans see an echo of Rhiannon in the Mari Lwyd, interpreting the journey from house to house of this Otherworldly, skeletal horse as representing her frantic search for her missing son. Ghostly and frightening during in the darkest time of the year, the mourning Divine Mother seeks the Divine Son, whose restoration to her is represented by the increasing light marked by the solstice.

That Rhiannon's horse was white is also significant, as there is almost an entire language of colors in medieval tales, and white was indisputably connected to the Otherworld; it is almost certain that the medieval audience would have immediately understood its connotations (Davies, 1997). As threshold guardians, white horses and their riders often play the role of psychopomp, and there are images of Epona from the continent which depict her riding a horse and holding a key, which is symbolic of her chthonic role, leading the deceased to the Otherworld.

However, Wood argues that unlike Epona or other equine divinities, Rhiannon's association with horses are related with punishment, rather than empowerment or queenship: she rides forth at the beginning of the First Branch in order to escape a marriage she does not want; for having allegedly eaten her newborn son, Rhiannon is punished by having to sit at a mounting block every day for seven years, where she offers to carry strangers on her back as a horse would; and in the Third Branch, she is abducted to the Otherworld and forced to wear an ass's collar around her neck — all of which was retaliation for the mistreatment of her rejected suitor Gwawl in the First Branch. These punishments, according to Wood, therefore disqualify her as being considered a sovereignty figure (Wood, 1997).

On the other hand, if we were to consider that the equine qualities exhibited by Rhiannon during these challenging episodes are not a mirror of her punishment but rather an indication of an imminent change of state or status, a different picture emerges, especially if we factor in the idea that the way in which the horse aspects manifest themselves is a reflection of where Rhiannon's power lies.

Winward proposes that, in general, the extent of power possessed by women as well as the strength of their presence in the narrative of *Y Mabinogi* is directly related to their marital status and life stage: when a woman is unpartnered or unmarried, she is at her most powerful, and not only do we hear her speak, we see her take an active role in the story. When she is married, both her personal power and the degree to which she speaks in the story are observably diminished. Finally, when she has become a mother, she possesses the least power, and she is more apt to be talked about than to speak for herself—if she doesn't disappear from the narrative completely, as women who become mothers in the *Mabinogi* tend to do (Winward, 1997).

These states of presence in the narrative are somewhat paralleled by the degree of autonomy a woman has at different points in her life, according to the medieval Welsh Laws of Women, which state that an unmarried woman is under the legal authority of her father, a married woman is under the legal authority of her husband, and if widowed, she comes under the legal authority of a son; should a woman not have one, legal authority over her reverts back to her father or family group (Cartwright, 2012).

When it comes to Rhiannon, we clearly see that when she is unmarried she is at the height of her power, both in word and deed. She defies the wishes of her father and takes action to ensure that she marries the man of her choosing. She reaches this goal after overcoming several challenges, including the complicated issue of honor that arose for Pwyll at their first marriage feast when he recklessly promised to give a supplicant anything within his power to give. Rhiannon deftly guides Pwyll to a clever solution in this situation which both keeps his honor intact as well as secures Rhiannon as his wife. During this transitional time between maiden and wife, Rhiannon's relationship to the horse is that she is its mistress and rider.

After Rhiannon's marriage to Pwyll, she goes to live with him in Dyfed, and becomes known as a very generous queen because of the gifts she bestows upon their courtiers. However, public opinion of her changes in time, and after three years of marriage without Rhiannon having birthed an heir, Pwyll's men encourage him to put her aside, something he refuses to do. And yet, even after she does give birth to a son, her nurses turn against her when the infant goes missing, and frame Rhiannon for the child's murder.

We clearly see here that after her marriage to Pwyll, Rhiannon exhibits less power. Where before Rhiannon was able to resolve complex issues of honor and hospitality through diplomacy and wit, after she is married has become a mother she is unable to convince those who framed her with infanticide to tell the truth of what happened. It is also significant that we do not see any conversation between Rhiannon and Pwyll regarding the loss of their child.

Instead, as required and expected, Rhiannon accepts the strange cruelty of Pwyll's punishment, which reflects both that she is now under the legal guardianship of her husband, as well as her relationship to the horse; by sitting daily at the mounting block and offering to carry strangers on her back, she performs the functions of a horse and so has effectively become one. Rhiannon transitions from wife to mother, and then from mother to childless mother in this part of the story. Her association with the liminal qualities of the horse are further underscored by the mirroring of the annual loss of Teyrnon's mare's foal, as well as the discovery of Rhiannon's newborn baby on the threshold of his home. The child himself is a mirror of the foal as they were both born on the same night—the threshold time of May Eve.

There is an international folk motif that features an Otherworldly "devouring mother" and a doubling of the "cannibalized" child with dogs. This plot point may have been an inclusion from outside influences from continental Europe, although it is more typical for this motif to feature the actual eating of animals instead of just the pretense of it having happened (Hemming, 1998). It is also interesting to note that images of Epona from the continent never depict her with a human child, but oftentimes depict the Goddess feeding foals, and sometimes her images also include dogs.

Finally, in the Third Branch, while Rhiannon does not feature as centrally to the tale, her sovereignty aspect is underscored by her acceptance of Manawydan as her husband. When Rhiannon and Pryderi are stolen away to the Otherworld, they experienced unusual punishments. Pryderi was made to wear door hammers, while Rhiannon was yoked with the collars of asses. This latter again alludes to her equine nature, and it is interesting that she again appears to embody the animal when she is separated from her mate, either by circumstance or by the status of their relationship. Not only had Rhiannon been kept in captivity and away from Manawydan for over a year, but the last time they saw each other, Rhiannon scolded Manawydan for being an unfaithful friend to her son before storming out to find the missing Pryderi, angry at her husband. That she found her voice to speak after her relative silence throughout the Third Branch recalls the agency and power of her maidenhood which she exhibited in the First Branch; yet her single-minded quest to rescue her son in the face of Manawydan's reticence mirrors both what she endured with her initial loss of Pryderi in infancy, as well as the gulf between herself and Pwyll during the course of her punishment for a crime she did not commit.

One of the hallmarks of the Sovereignty figure is that her form is a reflection of the status of the king to the land. When Rhiannon is out of synch or physically separated from her husband, she tends to exhibit equine characteristics which allude to her non-human origins and signify that there is an imbalance between the king and the land. That Dyfed undergoes a transformation that is similar to that of the Wasteland in the grail mythos is telling, as the grail itself is a proxy symbol for Sovereignty. Rhiannon's connection with the horse therefore is not a function of her punishment so much as it is a reflection of the status of her personal autonomy and marks her transition from one state of being to another. When Rhiannon exhibits her equine nature, it signifies that Sovereignty is starting to withdraw back into the land and, through it, to return to the Otherworldly origins of her power.

The Divine Queen

As modern readers, we may wonder why Rhiannon chose to abide by Pwyll's judgment of her, to ask why it is she didn't simply return home to the Otherworld. She was likely physically strong enough to do so; after all, she ostensibly carried some travelers on her back like a horse, and the story of the nurses that all six of them could not stop her from destroying her newborn baby was apparently believed by Pwyll and the judges, so clearly, the subtext is that she possessed some Otherworldly strength—strength enough, perhaps, to escape back to her own lands. That she chose to accept this judgment may be a reflection of the medieval layer of the narrative; this likely would have made perfect sense to the contemporary audience for several reasons.

One of the functions of myth is to illustrate, typically by means of cautionary example, the proper order of things, whether that concerns society, cosmology, or interpersonal relationships.

When things become disordered, when people especially act in a way that puts them outside of social balance and expectation, calamity is sure to strike. These tales, then, function as a moral template where the heroes strive to illustrate proper behavior in a given situation. As a queen, it would be expected for Rhiannon to obey the law of the land, and as the recipient of an unjust punishment—indeed serving as the very embodiment of the Calumniated Wife motif—Rhiannon not only illustrates lawfulness, but further distinguishes herself as someone of high moral character, even in the face of loss and injustice.

While the particular punishment enacted against Rhiannon is strange to the point that it likely can only reflect deep mythic origins, that Rhiannon was assessed this kind of redress at all is in keeping with medieval Welsh laws. It is interesting to note that Pwyll does not divorce Rhiannon, even at the behest of his court advisors; it appears therefore that she is still queen despite her daily requirement to sit by the mounting block outside of the gate of Arberth for seven years. There is no mention of imprisonment, and indeed, when Teyrnon, Gwri, and their retinue come to court, Rhiannon goes with them even though they refuse her offer of a ride on her back. Once there, she is seated beside Pwyll at the feast given in their guests' honor— even before Gwri is revealed as their missing son.

As we saw with Pwyll's misstep at his first wedding feast by too-readily agreeing to grant the supplicant Gwawl whatever he asked for, Rhiannon understands that there are social forms and contracts which must be adhered to, and it is especially important for the nobility to abide by these rules. Rhiannon illustrates an ability to work within the limitations of societal expectations, instead of breaking away from them altogether, which is the kind of behavior we see from both Aranrhod and Blodeuwedd in the Fourth Branch. Even when she appears at the Gorsedd Arberth to ask Pwyll if he would marry her, rather than having to marry someone she didn't love, Rhiannon was perfectly within her legal right to do so, as medieval Welsh law did not permit families to give women away in marriage against their will.

It is this shrewdness of understanding that the law is in place for a reason and that everyone, noble or otherwise, is beholden to it that reflects so well on Rhiannon's moral character. It follows to say that as a Sovereignty figure, Rhiannon is the very embodiment of this social construct, and so can do nothing less but to adhere to it. And so, resigned to her fate, Rhiannon chooses to work within the social construct and accept her punishment, proving herself to be a great and noble lady, whose perseverance is rewarded when her child is at last returned to her and her innocence proven. Rhiannon, as a wife and mother, is no longer the autonomous woman of her maidenhood, and now demonstrates by example, the behavior that is expected of the medieval Welsh woman. "The virtues to be fostered are patience, modesty, wisdom, chastity, loyalty—these are the virtues that will ultimately win the day" (Davies, pg. 80, 1993).

Chapter Six

Seeking Her Within

Throughout this book, we have explored the myths, symbols, and attributions of Rhiannon. It is my belief that this information is crucial to help build a relationship with this beautiful divinity, especially since her stories were not written down by those who actively worshiped her. In one respect, this puts modern Pagans and Polytheists who are drawn to work with Rhiannon and other British divinities at a disadvantage because we do not have access to the types of resources available to Pagans who work with Gods and Goddesses from cultures who themselves have recorded the myths, rituals, prayers, and details of worship of their divinities.

On the other hand, because myth depicts Rhiannon as a fairy queen—less than a Goddess but ostensibly more than a human—her story is somewhat more relatable than those of divinities who are engaged with more cosmological concerns. In Rhiannon, we see a woman in process. She experiences challenges, trials, and losses just like anyone, and certainly many of us have experienced the same losses that she has. This relatability permits us to connect with Rhiannon in a way that reflects her ability to understand the human condition. This accessibility allows us to call to Rhiannon in times of need.

She is the Great Mother whose understanding and compassion is infinite and whose love is fierce and unconditional. Hers is the broad back of the mare that bears us through the darkest of times and over the rockiest of terrain. It is she who teaches us how to endure the challenges of life and bears us forth into the presence of our Sovereignty, permitting us to shift from one reality to another. She is the guardian of the liminal threshold that moves us from one situation to another, from one life stage to another... and from the present manifestation of who we are

Reflecting Sovereignty Within

Shakespeare said that art is a mirror held up to nature. And that's what it is. The nature is your nature, and all of these wonderful poetic images of mythology are referring to something in you. When your mind is trapped by the image out there so that you never make the reference to yourself, you have misread the image. Joseph Campbell, *The Power of Myth*

While the type of refection Campbell is speaking about doesn't mean that the Gods exist only (or simply) as archetypes or psychological constructs, it can nevertheless be very informative to reflect their tales inward. This provides us with a process that helps us discover what parts of any myth resonate with our own stories, as well as insight as to how these sacred stories can help inform our spiritual paths and catalyze our personal process.

One way of looking at Rhiannon therefore is as a representation of our Sovereign Self that comes up into consciousness from the subconscious realm of the Otherworld, pursuing that which it most desires. We can try to track our authentic selves down and chase after our dreams, but it is only in truly engaging them — naming these goals and asking for what we need — do they reveal themselves to us. It is a long process to manifest and integrate our Sovereign Self—to wed it to our "good sense" and help to develop the ability to hear the truth of its wisdom—because there are challenges to overcome. We have to process loss, and mourn for what we had hoped our lives would be, and we often find ourselves trapped in destructive patterns that cause us to feel "othered" or disconnected from the core truth of who and what we are.

We can become so invested in carrying the heavy loads of

our emotional and physical responsibilities, which often include bearing the needs and expectations of others, that we allow our strengths to be drained and our resources to be used up, leaving nothing left for ourselves. What Sovereignty wants and needs when it does rise up from the Otherworld of the unconscious, is to dwell completely in a person's consciousness; it seeks to be to be embodied. It is a great test of personal Sovereignty for us to learn how to remain authentically who we are, no matter the challenges or circumstances around us.

Just as Rhiannon is sought after by Pwyll, the active mind seeks to integrate the wisdom of the lessons it has learned—it is our conscious self seeking an authentic experience, no matter the potential risks to the status quo of the present moment. Pryderi can be seen as the result of the union of Sovereignty and consciousness, the wondrous child that represents the birth of the new self, when that which is sought has come into manifestation. The challenge here lies in keeping present in this new life… keeping grounded in a new sense of self, and centered in self-worth. Rhiannon teaches us to endure in the face of persecution, regardless of the of lack of support from those who will not themselves take responsibility for their own lives, and despite those doubts and fears that rise up from within us— trying to convince us that we are not worthy of what we seek to have, who we strive to be, and all we hope to accomplish.

When we can do this, and live from this powerful and conscious center, nothing can move us from our mark.

We will be Sovereign.

We will be free.

The Functions of Rhiannon

Based upon what we have glimpsed both explicitly in the stories where she appears, and implicitly through a close reading of these same texts—and perhaps with a sprinkling of folk tradition mixed in, even if there is no proof of any direct lineage to ancient

Celtic Pagan practices—here are some of the spiritual functions of Rhiannon and ways in which to approach her.

Rhiannon as Lady of the Land

In this iteration, she is a Sovereignty Goddess, testing and choosing the candidate who would best serve as king. She rides forth on a White Mare, indicating her Otherworldly origins, while also keeping watch over her domain. She connects this world with the Otherworld, and as such, serves as a bridge or a threshold between the two. By reflecting these ideas within, we can see the liminal qualities of the horse as bridging the conscious, waking world with the unconscious, intuitive world. Rhiannon not only guides our way from one state of being to another, she also carries us on her back if we need support during difficult times. She teaches us how to obtain our Sovereignty—which I define in the context of the inner landscape as "fully-conscious self-determination"—by learning to ask for that which we need. Rhiannon also demonstrates the importance of being true to what you know to be your authentic and Sovereign self, even in the face of doubt and persecution from the outside world. As Lady of the Land, Rhiannon is a granter of abundance, and her magical bag which cannot be filled is, in many ways, a proxy both of the dish or cornucopia filled with food that we see in images of Epona, and a resonance of the Cauldron of Abundance and Transformation.

Rhiannon as Lady of the Otherworld

In this more subtle iteration, Rhiannon is a faerie bride who brings great magic with her to this world. She rides out from the Gorsedd Arberth, a mound where one will receive blows or see a great wonder—exactly the type of mound that would be considered a doorway to the Otherworld. Rhiannon is dressed in a silk brocade that symbolizes her Otherworldly origins, and she appears to play the role of the psychopomp—a guide who assists the spirits of the dead to cross the threshold into the Otherworld. The latter ties into the liminal qualities of her white mare, whose very color is a hallmark of the Otherworld, as well as with the Adar Rhiannon, the three magical birds which, like most things associated with the Otherworld, appear able to warp human perceptions of space and time. In "Culhwch and Olwen" these same birds are said to be able to soothe the souls of the living and awaken the souls of the dead. When reflected within, Rhiannon's role as Lady of the Otherworld calls us to transform those parts of ourselves which no longer serve us, to dare to pass over the threshold that leads us from one state of being to the next, all the while promising us that, even in the face of our greatest pain and deepest sorrow, the song of her birds will bring us comfort and the blessing of forgetting our troubles—even if for a little while.

Rhiannon as the Divine Mother

Perhaps the most poignant and relatable attributes of Rhiannon are connected to her role as Mother. It is after the loss of her newborn son, and the unjust punishment she receives when the child's negligent nurses blame her for his loss, that we witness Rhiannon's deeply sympathetic character and endless compassion. She assures the nurses that no harm will come to them if they tell the truth of what happened to the child, and when they refuse, Rhiannon bravely and with dignity accepts Pwyll's punishment. Here, then, is a divinity who is intimately acquainted with the loss of a child, and who knows what it means to have to carry an unjust burden.

We can also imagine Rhiannon's pain in the Third Branch when she learns that her son has disappeared again. She takes Manawydan to task for having lost Pryderi and leaving him behind, before setting forth to find him for herself. Although her attempt to free Pryderi from the magical fortress results in her own entrapment, and they are both are taken to the Otherworld for punishment, we see in Rhiannon a fierce and selfless mother-figure whose love for her child transcends all. Reflecting this within, whether one is a literal parent or someone who is devoted to birthing a project or a life which is in accordance with their greatest desires and highest purpose, Rhiannon models our need for dedication to our work and loyalty to our vision. She embodies the pureness of unconditional love, and, as her children, gathers us up into her arms, and holds us as we move through the pain of our losses. She opens our hearts, and teaches us to love and mother ourselves as fiercely as she, the Divine Mother, loves us.

Rhiannon as Calumniated Wife

Gentle but firm, Rhiannon shows us that she knows what it is to be "Other", knows how to endure an unspeakable loss, and knows what it feels like to suffer an unjust punishment. When reflected within, we can see how Rhiannon also demonstrates that regardless of what challenges and life situations come our way, if we can endure the hardships and the heartaches while staying true to who and what we are from a place of inner sovereignty and personal authenticity, then in the end, our faith in ourselves will pay off and we will obtain that which we most desire.

The Lessons of Rhiannon

Rhiannon teaches us that:

- We have the power to choose our Sovereign natures over our learned fears.
- We have the strength to endure in the face of grave injustice.
- We have the ability to change our shape—to transform ourselves and our lives.
- We have the vision to be able to move through suffering and loss and into redemption.

Rhiannon encourages us to:

- Ask for what we need.

- Stay committed to our truths.
- Persevere in the face of challenge.
- Pursue what we love and what will make us most fulfilled.
- Seek comfort and solace to ease our way; the lap of the Mother welcomes all.
- Bear our burdens with grace, and ask for help when needed; we need not carry them alone.

Chapter Seven

Building a Relationship with Rhiannon

If we step outside of the realms of mythology and history, it is clear that the memory of Rhiannon persists in modern pop culture. Most people are familiar with the Stevie Nicks song "Rhiannon", which was inspired by a novel called *Triad*, by Mary Leader. While the book itself only made vague references to Welsh myth, Nicks was stunned at how well the song she wrote reflected the story of Rhiannon when she read the *Mabinogi* after the fact. Nicks wrote another song, called "Angel" which she said is directly influenced by the Rhiannon of the *Mabinogi*. Other groups, including Faith and the Muse and Faun, have written songs inspired by Rhiannon, and she features in the movie *Otherworld,* an animated retelling of the Four Branches. But perhaps the most well-known retelling is that of Evangeline Walton, whose *Mabinogion Tetralogy* lays out Rhiannon's story in *The Prince of Annwn* and *The Song of Rhiannon*.

The modern Pagan movement has played a huge role in restoring Rhiannon to a place of honor by recognizing her divinity. She features prominently in the pantheons of established traditions such as the Anglesey Druid Order and the Sisterhood of Avalon, as well as being honored in the devotional work of Brythonic Polytheists, Welsh Reconstructionists, Druidic practitioners, and individual Pagans of many types and traditions. There are many ways to approach this Goddess, both in the context of a formal tradition as well as on the path of an inspired individual. What follows therefore are some devotional practices that anyone who feels drawn to Rhiannon can use in order to build or deepen a meaningful and authentic relationship with the Divine Queen.

Shrines and Altars

Setting up a devotional shrine or creating a place to honor Rhiannon on your working altar is a powerful way to invite her presence into your life. When creating any shrine, it can be helpful to meditate on the symbols associated with the divinity you are seeking to honor, and begin to gather those items or images together in a space dedicated to them. The Hermetic Principle of Correspondence which teaches that "like attracts like" underscores this practice; the more the images, symbols, and cultural components hold or replicate your understanding of the deity in question, the more the shrine can act to build a connection between you and the God/dess to whom it is dedicated.

Shrines can be of any size, ranging from an elaborately carved piece of furniture, to a shelf on a wall or in a bookcase, an assemblage of wall art, or even a collage of meaningful images. You can decide if you want to include an image of Rhiannon on her shrine, perhaps in the form of a piece of devotional art or sculpture made by you or purchased elsewhere. There are several commercially available statues of Rhiannon to choose from, including reproductions of ancient Epona statuary which may resonate with you. Alternatively, you may find something depicting a horsewoman that speaks to Rhiannon's energy for you, or else choose instead to represent her with an image of a white mare.

My personal shrine to Rhiannon incorporates several statuary images of her, a large banner with an image of her from the "Avalonian Oracle" deck; a small pottery figure of a white horse that I purchased in Wales, a resin box carved with white knotwork horses which contains a vial of a vibrational elixir I made on pilgrimage at the site of Rhiannon's court in Narberth, a leather bag embossed with knotwork, a stone with triple black birds intertwined with knots, a rock I picked up on the Gorsedd Arberth, an antique horseshoe, a small iron cauldron with a triple horse broach leaning against it where I burn herbs in her honor, and a pottery dish to receive offerings I leave for Rhiannon. For me, the difference between shrines and working altars is that shrines serve as a daily reminder of our devotion to our Gods. Whenever I pass my Rhiannon shrine, the images and energies I've build up there help me to connect and fortify my relationship with her, reinforce the intentions of the work I've been doing with her, and remind me to take a moment to be present in her presence, no matter how hectic my day may be.

Here are some correspondences for Rhiannon primarily gathered from her stories in *Y Mabinogi* which may be of use to you in putting together your own shrine to the Goddess:

- *Symbols*: White mare, three black birds, bag, golden veil, mare and foal, hanging cauldron, horse block, yoke, moon, torc.
- *Animals*: White mare, three black birds, dogs and puppies, badger.
- *Colors*: White, gold (attested in text); red (fertility, smeared blood, associated with the Otherworld along with the color white).

Offerings

A powerful way to give thanks to the Gods and to show them honor is to present them with an offering; these offerings can take many forms. As in ancient days, offerings can be gifts in the form of food, libations, herbs, flowers, stones, and other items. These can be placed on house altars and shrines and later brought outside and placed under a tree, in a body of water if appropriate, committed to a bonfire, and even buried in the ground. Choosing what to give as an offering can be as simple as giving what feels right to you, or as involved as researching the kinds of things ancient peoples would have gifted these Gods and then seeking out those items, or their modern equivalents.

The Celts where known to create votive deposits, often

gifting high status items such as swords, horse trappings, and cauldrons to the Gods; as they believed that water was a gateway to the Otherworld, we have found large collections of offerings in lakes or at the source of rivers. Often, these offerings were created specifically to be given to the Gods, and were broken before being deposited, likely as part of the ritual, rendering them useless to humans. In Wales, one famous votive deposit was discovered in the lake waters of Llyn Cerrig Bach. It is also believed that in times of great need, the Celts performed human sacrifices in hopes that the departed would bring the appeal of the people before the Gods directly.

While of course we would never perform human sacrifice today, the idea of an offering representing a sacrifice is a powerful one. The very word means "to make sacred", and we can transform something into a sacrifice when we imbue it with intention and make it meaningful. Some say that a sacrifice should have an impact on the one who is offering it; this can be achieved by gifting something one has worked hard to obtain or an item which holds great emotional attachment. Tossing a tumbled stone one has just purchased into a lake with intention as an offering can be meaningful, but thanking the Gods for a blessing they have given you with the gift of a pinky ring you've worn since childhood, for example, holds a different devotional impact.

Offerings do not always have to be things; one can thank or honor the Gods with the gift of your time and energy. Creating a devotional piece of art or music is a powerful offering, as is volunteering your time in support of a charity or donating goods and services to a cause which is in alignment with the divinity you are seeking to honor. You can commit yourself to learning a skill, engaging in an activity, or adopting a moral code which you feel would please the Goddess. Offerings of the self are the most powerful ways to engage with the divine because they are often the most intimate. I personally tend to not see offerings as part of an exchange economy, where they are given in order to procure a desired outcome with the help of deity; rather, I think offerings are best used as a method of building a relationship with our Gods—a show of dedication, discipline, and devotion.

Here are some ideas for offerings you can gift to Rhiannon:

- *Food*: Welsh cakes, apples, honey, mead, apple cider.
- *Plants*: Rose, red clover, lady's mantle, and motherwort. These can decorate the altar, be placed in a dish as your offering, or burned together on a charcoal disk as a devotional incense.
- *Items*: Horse trappings, horse shoes, black bird feathers, bag.
- *Service*: Rehabilitating and rescuing horses (or supporting organizations that do this work); working to help missing and exploited children; sharing music therapeutically with those in need of serenity and joy; working with or donating to organizations that advocate for women's rights, safety, and well-being; working with dogs at an animal shelter.

When I am actively working at my shrine, I light candles and burn incense to empower my intention and to honor the Goddess, and I will often leave seven- day candles burning on the shrine to represent whatever intention I placed before Rhiannon in my work. I sometimes place live flowers on my shrine as a gift or a token of gratitude, and often place things like herbs, stones, and pieces of fruit in the offering dish; depending on what is in it, I have an outdoor shrine where I eventually place the offerings I've left for any of the deities I work with. I do this once a moon for non-perishable offerings, and the next day when I leave offerings of food.

Journey Work: Rhiannon Trance Posture

Inspired by the work of Felicitas Goodman, ecstatic trance postures are inner journeying tools that permit seekers to have an experience which leads to understanding through the embodiment of a figure, artifact, symbol or even natural phenomenon, such as a landscape feature or a tree.

While there are no known ancient depictions of Rhiannon, the abundance of devotional images of the goddess Epona have a very strong resonance with our initial meeting with Rhiannon in the First Branch: that of a noble female figure serenely riding a horse with an unhurried gait. Although in the *Mabinogi* Rhiannon is not described as holding anything as she rides before the Goresdd Arberth, images of Epona often depict her holding a basket of food or a torc of sovereignty. Rhiannon is described as riding with her head covered with a golden veil, and later on in the First Branch she gives a magical bag to Pwyll which can never be filled. While Rhiannon's riding style is not specified in the text, almost every image of Epona depicts her as riding side-saddle; she presents with her entire body facing forward, while her mount is viewed from its side beneath her.

None of this is meant to infer that Epona and Rhiannon are the same divinity, but there is little question that they have many similarities, and may perhaps be related. That said, even without drawing upon the iconography of Epona, the author of the *Mabinogi* certainly provides us with enough of a descriptive image of Rhiannon that we can easily imagine her as an unhurried horsewoman astride her gently walking, white horse. For this embodiment exercise, you can choose to rely solely upon the textual description of Rhiannon, or research and emulate one of the various icons of Epona to use as the basis for this posture. In the latter case, instead of a bowl or basket of food, you can choose to hold or visualize yourself holding a bag or sack in order to tie more fully into the energies of Rhiannon specifically. You may also consider draping a scarf or wrap over your head to represent Rhiannon's veil.

There are many ways to approach trance posture work, and many types of information which this tool can provide. Primarily, trance postures are a powerful way to come to understand the image, symbol, or in this case, personage being embodied. When taking a posture journey, setting up your intention beforehand will set the tone of your work and specify what you are seeking to learn.

Performing a Rhiannon trance posture can help you to connect with the Goddess so you can ask her questions directly: you can enquire about her and ways to honor in order to deepen your relationship with her; you can ask her for clarity about her symbols or parts of her story—for example, asking why she accepted the unjust punishment for a crime she did not commit; and you can ask her for guidance in your own life and spiritual process.

Embodying this posture can help you integrate some of Rhiannon's lessons and bring insight into ways you can be sovereign in your own life; teach you how to bear the burdens of life and its injustices with grace and inner strength born of certainty, anchored in your own truth; comfort you in times of deep loss and sorrow; and help you to connect with the inner strength necessary to support others in your life with as much unconditional love as possible.

The Map of the Journey

Follow these steps to undertake a trance posture journey:
1. Set aside quiet time to yourself.
2. Wear loose and comfortable clothing.
3. Work in your sacred space, surrounded by those things that trigger entrance into the realm of the spiritual. The simple act of spreading a sarong on the ground dedicated solely for use in these workings can help move you into a

receptive space for journeying.

4. Be sure you know how to embody the posture before you begin.

5. Have any necessary props or posture aids gathered and accessible.

6. Clear and center, coming to a neutral energy space before beginning your work.

7. Sit and clear your mind by paying attention to your breath for at least 15 minutes before embodying the posture.

8. Embody the posture as detailed below. If you are going to wear a veil, place it over your head before you begin.

9. Accompany the posture with an audio recording of 15 minutes of Trance Drumming. These are readily available on the internet; be sure to choose one that has a call-back beat at the end so that you know it is time to complete your work. Research has found that a drumming rhythm of 200-210 beats per minute seems to trigger the nervous system to enter the altered state of consciousness desired for these postures. If you cannot find a drumming track that you like, or if you prefer silence, focus on the rhythm of your breath as you journey and set a gentle alarm for 15 minutes from your starting time.

10. Start the drumming track, and be sure to keep your focus clear as you journey, while still allowing insight to flow. Spend the entire length of the 15 minutes of drumming (or breathing) remaining as clear and as open to the experience as you can. Pay attention to any and all visions, scenes, emotions, insights or information presented to you.

Rhiannon Posture Instructions

• Sit on a chair or couch with knees bent, legs closed and parallel to each other, and both feet flat on the floor.

- Envision your seat as a serene white horse upon which you are sitting side saddle. Her head is on your left side and she looks steadily forward in that direction, with her left leg raised as if ready to take a step.
- Your back is straight, your torso upright, your shoulders back, and your head facing forward.
- Your left arm is outstretched and your hand is resting on the "neck" of your "horse". A high pillow or bolster placed beside you can make this position more comfortable as well as help it feel more real.
- Your right hand rests lightly in your lap, or alternatively can be holding an apple, a bag, a bowl, or a torc.
- Start the drumming track.
- Close your eyes. Suspend disbelief. Release expectation. Ask Rhiannon to be with you as you journey. Go...

After the Journey

It is always important to ground and center after every posture session. Release any excess energy or emotions that may have come up for you during the posture process. Place your hands on the ground and breathe those energies out until you feel centered and balanced. If you find it hard to get grounded, breathe up some rich, green Earth energy from the planet to help you find your center. It is unusual for people performing these postures to feel imbalanced, but it is better to know what to do than to feel unprepared.

Be sure to journal your experiences; make a written record of everything you heard, saw, and felt during your journey. These self-reflective questions can help you process your experience:

- How did the posture make you feel?
- What would you name this posture?
- What is the lesson of this posture?
- How does it relate to you and your process?

- What does this posture bring up for you?
- What did you learn about Rhiannon from performing this posture?
- What did you learn about yourself?
- In what way has this posture helped you to connect with Rhiannon?
- What is your next step in building a relationship with her?
- Know that this posture is something you can do over and over again. It is a powerful and effective tool, and it is worth developing this skill through practice. Each time you perform this posture, you can bring a different question with you, setting up your intention clearly before you begin. Remember one of the great lessons that Rhiannon has to teach us: ask for what you need.

Devotional Chants, Prayers, and Invocations

While I have collected a few of these devotional writings and songs, I encourage you to create your own as you move into relationship with Rhiannon.

Invocation to Rhiannon

Holy Rhiannon, Lady of the Otherworld, fill me with your boundless Love and endless compassion. Great Queen, teach me to ask for that which I most need and to endure the trials set before me on the path to obtaining that which I most desire. Nurturing Mother, help me to bear my burdens with strength and grace so that, empowered and empowering, I may in turn serve others.

Affirmation of the Divine Queen

I know who I am, what I need, and what I have to give. I live from my sovereign center, and take strength from the truth of my inner wisdom. I meet every challenge with clarity, and can see the gifts of growth they bring to me. There is nothing I cannot endure, and no place I must go alone. Broad-backed Rhiannon gives me the strength I need to move through any challenge, while her sweet-singing birds comfort my soul.

Rhiannon Chant

(Em) The White Mare (D) dances in the (Em) Ninth Wave's foam
(G)Call out Her (D) name and (Em) She'll bear you (D)home
To the (G)Other (D)world where (Em) Her birds still (D)sing,
(Em) soothing your (D)soul with their (Em) song
The (G) Silver (D) Branch is the (Em) Scepter of the Great Queen, (D)Rhiannon. (Em)

Swift White Horse
by Tammi Boudreau

Chorus:
(Em) Ride a (D)swift white (Em) horse, oh (D)Mother,
(Em)Ride a (D)swift white (Em)horse.
(Em)Though the (D) path seems (Em) dark and (Am)troubled
(C)Stay fast (D) to your (Em) course.

Once You wed a king, dear Mother,
Once You wed a king.
Bore a son and bore a burden,
So the Three Birds sing.

Chorus

Truth comes in full time, my Mother,
Truth comes in full time.
Harvest now the seeds we've planted,
Branch and earth and vine.

Chorus x 2

Though the path seems dark and troubled—
Stay fast to your course.

Invocation
by Kelly Woo

Rhiannon, Divine Queen,
Lady of Manifestation and Mystery,
Bathed in Golden Light,
You ride forth from the Otherworld,
Strong in Self, Rooted in Love,
Untameable as the wind,
Upon which your birds fly high.
I ask that you stand with me,
Supporting me in my struggles,
And lending me your strength and grace,
That I may overcome and uncover the Great Queen Within.

Chant to Rhiannon
by Kelly Woo

Lady, please listen
Stay for awhile
Challenges burden
And Shadows beguile
Great Queen of Mysteries
Through thick and through thin
Help me stand true
To the Sovereign Within

Chapter Eight

Rhiannon Speaks

I have been a priestess in service to Rhiannon for over 20 years, and I consciously worked to make the writing of this book a devotional act. When the first draft was complete, I stood at my altar and invoked Rhiannon. With pen and notebook in hand, I asked her if there was anything more she wanted for me to include; if there was anything she wished to say to those who would read this book… to YOU, now holding it. What follows is the result of what became an automatic writing session; I have only edited it slightly for clarity, and tried to retain the shape of it as much as possible. I humbly submit this to you, recorded as accurately as possible, and ask that you keep in mind that this has come through a flawed vessel who has tried to get out of her own way in order to hear the words of the Divine Queen, and beloved Mother, as clearly as possible. And so…

Rhiannon Speaks:

I come to you in this Now time, the threshold Between where all is sacred… always on that precipice between what Was and what may Be. What Is, is that place—that time—the Now where all changes go. To pursue the fair prize of the Wonder is to never touch it, for you cannot by its nature; to remain in fear of the Blows, you cannot escape its sting. Caught in dream, lost in fear, the Now slips by and the bag can never be filled.

You who would follow me must be prepared to wear the ass's collar… to be whisked away into the Otherworld of pain and growth and silence to forge a self with many hammers. The Wondrous Youth is your sovereign self—the next king to be— the next part of the self that needs to be birthed forth.

I am the Great Divine Mother. The Nurturing One. The

Threshold Guardian. I birth and I receive: the womb and the tomb are mine. My strength carries you through each portal, stands waiting for you at each threshold — not just those of death and of life, but also of new beginnings and of the releasing of old ties.

The steady gait of the milk-white Steed of the Moon, of the Bounty of the Breast — this is the elixir that heals the Wasteland. This is what frees the prisoner, for it is when you leave my breast, it is when you have forgotten who you are, that you dwell in the ancient prison of your own design.

You must move through the sentries of these layers, through the threshold of these mysteries: the blackbird, the stag, the owl, the eagle, and the salmon.

This last is the wisdom that will unlock the gate and set the prisoner free. That prisoner is the Wondrous Child... YOU. Heir of the Abundant Mother of the Earth. Next in line from the lineage of Ancestors, from the Otherworld of their memory.

Your father, also Wisdom, the King of the Otherworld, Master of the Past, of what lies Within, of what has come Before. He battles himself at the ford, in the waters of the Within... there at the threshold of summer and winter, of knowing and wisdom, of consciousness and unconsciousness. One blow is all that is needed. The Sword, the Spear, the Blade of Truth rings through, and you emerge victorious. Child of the Father... your own child, your own father.

And I... I will sanctify you, reinforce your victory, reconsecrate your sovereignty. The cost is constant renewal, oh my child! The battle is yearly, for the next prisoner needs to be freed. Seek out the Guardians of the inner temple: the Oldest Animals, the inner instinct that knows, if not the truth of who you are and where dwells your sovereignty, but then at least the places you can find them — where to look.

Temper your impulse with wisdom. Do not jump too quickly into the unknown, but also do not deprive yourself of opportunity for fear's sake. The greatest wisdoms lay in the

Cauldron of Rebirth—four chains uphold it. And when you've entered its fortress, you must pause. You cannot speak of the Mysteries. They are for you alone. Be aware of the signs and follow your instincts. Learn the difference between fear of change and growth, and the fear that is triggered because of danger and deception.

Think too on that which you truly need: how big of a bag must you carry? There is honor in hard work and your crown is not tarnished by it. It is only when you bow to the fear and illusions of others that the torc begins to unwind. When you can make peace, make peace. Your personal sovereignty is threatening to others when you do not play by their rules, when you excel and succeed because you have been true to who and what you are. Be wary, but be compassionate. Do not turn the tools of Art into weapons, for even if you defeat your enemies in combat, it is they who will have won.

Honor yourself by honoring your word. Fulfill your commitments as best you can and do not be afraid to ask for help. Even if the world shifts and you no longer recognize the landscape around you, seek to be grounded in the landscape within you. Find the tools you need to re-craft your life.

Be generous with your bounty.
Be clear and careful with your words.
Be true to your vision.
Be honorable in your actions.
Be grounded in your sovereignty.
Be welcome in my presence.
    I of the broad back to carry you.
    I of the sweet song to comfort you.
    I of the wide lap to nurture you.
    I of the deep bag to fortify you.
    I of the threshold to
        LEAD YOU HOME.

Love yourself and others.
Forgive yourself and others.

The past is your teacher.
The future is your student.

The present is the threshold between.

Step through every moment.
Step through each breath.
Step through the space between each heartbeat.

Where you stand is ever the bridge.
    How you cross this moment,
    What you choose to bring with you,
    Where you land on the other side...
        This is the burden of sovereignty.

And if where you land has pain unavoidable—loss, hurt,
injury, death—how we step through is what we can control:
        the way we carry the burden,
        the companions we choose to walk with us,
        the tools within us to help us move through,
        the release of the struggle so that we are open to
        learn,
            open to yet love, open to face the truth
            of the prison,
            and seek how to set our wonder child
            free once again.

We are not born to suffer, to carry shame, to live in fear.
We are born to remember our sovereignty, to find healing in
the pain, release in the shame, love in the fear.
To harness the challenges—the disappointment, the loss, the

hurt, the fear, the pain.

To move through them.

To use them as a bridge to understanding, a pathway to increased sovereignty, a KEY to unlock the door of your inner prison.

The challenges are not the endpoint. We aren't meant to dwell there.

They are the THRESHOLD over which we are meant to step, the bridge we are meant to cross, the boundary we are meant to break through.

For on the other side of it is the joy of release, of freedom, of the renewal.

>the reunion of Mother and Child,
>of self to source,
>of emptiness to wholeness.

The burden is lifted.

And we are free.

And sovereign.

I am the swift steed.

I am the law of right rule.

I am the door that swings into life and into death.

I am the pathway to the chieftain's court.

I am the key that frees the sacred prisoner.

I am the mother that births the warrior.

I am she who receives him home again.

Who receives YOU home again.

Conclusion

The Journey Begins

Through overgrown pathways of history that twist and bend, and lead out of sight, we have sought her. Through the living words captured in the black finality of ink on the candlelit illumination of precious vellum, we have chased her down. Through a webbed lineage of far-flung divinities, some anchored in a past unknowable, some revealing themselves in layers like a nesting doll with the truth of her at its core, we have made desperate pursuit.

And through it all, in the end, the lesson remains this: No matter the provenance. No matter the proof. No matter the mastery of the lore, or the availability of the resources, or the correctness of the translation. In order for Rhiannon to reveal herself to you... for you to come to know the truth of her... for you to be in right relationship with the Divine Queen and with your own Sovereignty... only one thing is needed. Only one thing must be done.

Ask.

And she will stop.

And she will answer.

Appendix 1

Notes on Welsh Pronunciation

VOWELS

a short: pronounced as in pan.

a long: pronounced as in father.

e short: pronounced as in pen.

e long: pronounced like the first element of the diphthong in lane.

i short: pronounced as in pin.

i long: pronounced as in machine.

o short: pronounced as in cot.

o long: pronounced like the first element of the diphthong in note.

u: pronounced (approximately) like the French u in sur.

w short: pronounced like the oo in wood.

w long: pronounced like the oo in wooed.

y: pronounced sometimes like u in but, and sometimes (approximately) like the French u in sur.

DIPHTHONGS

They may be pronounced by giving to each of the component vowels the value indicated above.

CONSONANTS

c is always pronounced as k, chi as in the Scotch loch, dd as th in breathe, f as v, ff as f, s is always hard, as in loss; ll represents a spirant l, a very difficult sound to represent in English— Englishmen generally render it as thl.

ACCENT

The accent is nearly always on the last syllable but one (or penult) as Elidyr, Seithényn.

EXAMPLES

Gwyddno = Gwithno, th as in breathe; Gwenhúdiw = Gwenhid-
ue; Syfáddon = Syváthon, th as in breathe; Dwt = D?ot, oo as
in wood; Pwca = P?oka, oo as in wood; Ardúdwy = Ardid?oi;
Llwyd = Ll??id, ll the spirant l, oo as in wooed.

(From *The Welsh Fairy Book*, by Jenkin W. Thomas)

Bibliography

Primary Sources

Apuleius, Lucius, Adlington, W., trans., *The Golden Ass: being the metamorphoses of Lucius Apuleius* (London: William Heinemann, 1922).

Babbit, Frank Cole, trans., *Plutarch's Moralia* (Cambridge, MA: Harvard University Press, 1936).

Bollard, John K., trans., *The Mabinogi: Legend and Landscape of Wales* (Llandysul: Gomer Press Limited, 2006).

Bromwich, Rachel, ed. and trans., *Trioedd Ynys Prydein: The Welsh Triads* (Cardiff: University of Wales Press 2006).

Bromwich, Rachel and Evans, D. Simon, trans., *Culhwch and Olwen: An Edition and Study of the Oldest Arthurian Tale,* (Cardiff: University of Wales Press, 1992).

Coe, Jon B., and Young, Simon, The Celtic Source for the Arthurian Legend, (Felinfach: Llanerch Publishers, 1995).

* Davies, Sioned, trans., *The Mabinogion* (New York: Oxford University Press, 2007).

Ford, Patrick K., trans., *The Mabinogi and Other Medieval Welsh Tales* (California: University of California Press, 1977).

Gray, Elizabeth A., *Cath Maige Tuired: Second Battle of Mag Tuired* (Dublin: Irish Texts Society, 1983).

Guest, Charlotte, trans., *The Mabinogion* (London: Richard Clay and Sons, Ltd., 1906).

Gwynn, Edward, trans., *The Metrical Dindshenchas,* (Dublin: Royal Irish Academy House, 1903).

McDevitte, W.A, trans., Bohn, W.S., trans., *Caesar's Gallic War,* (New York: Harper & Brothers, 1869).

O'Meara, John J., *Gerald of Wales: The History and Topography of Ireland,* (Dundalgan Press, 1951)

Parker, Will, trans., *The Four Branches of the Mabinogi* (California: Bardic Press, 2005).

*Preferred academic translation.

Secondary Sources

Beck, Noémie, "Goddesses in Celtic Religion, Cult and Mythology: A Comparative Study of Ancient Ireland, Britain and Gaul", (Unpublished Ph.D. Thesis, University College Dublin, 2009)

Breeze, Andrew, *The Origins of the Four Branches of the Mabinogi* (Herfordshire, Gracing Press, 2009)

Cartwright, Jane, *Women in the Middle Ages: Sources from the Celtic Regions*, (Lampeter: University of Wales, 2012).

Cunliffe, Barry, *The Ancient Celts*, (Oxford: Oxford University Press, 1997).

Davies, Sioned, *The Four Branches of the Mabinogi* (Llandysul: Gomer Press, 1993).

Davies, Sioned, "Horses in the *Mabinogion*", *The Horse in Celtic Culture: Medieval Welsh Perspectives,* Jones, Nerys Ann, and Davies, Sioned, eds., (Cardiff: University of Wales Press, 1997), 121 – 140

Derks, Ton, *Gods, Temples and Ritual Practice: The Transformation of Religious Ideas and Values in Roman Gaul (Amsterdam Archaeological Studies),* (Amsterdam: Amsterdam University Press, 1998)

Dexter, Miriam Robbins, "The Hippomorphic Goddess and Her Offspring", *Journal of Indo-European Studies,* (1990), 285 – 307

Dunbar, Agnes B.C., *A Dictionary of Saintly Women*, (London: George Bell and Sons, 1905).

Ford, Patrick K., "Prolegomena to a Reading of the "Mabinogi": 'Pwyll' and 'Manawydan'",
Studia Celtica, 16/17 (1981/1982), 110

Findon, Joanne, *A Woman's Words: Emer and Female Speech in the Ulster Cycle*, (Toronto: University of Toronto Press, 1997).

Garman, Alex, *The Cult of the Matronae in the Roman Rhineland: An Historical Evaluation of the Archaeological Evidence* (New York:

Edwin Mellen Press, 2008).

Green, Miranda Aldhouse, "The Symbolic Horse in Pagan Celtic Europe: An Archaeological Perspective", *The Horse in Celtic Culture: Medieval Welsh Perspectives,* Davies, Sioned and Jones, Nerys Ann, eds., (Cardiff: University of Wales Press, 1997), 1 – 22

Gruffydd, W.J., *Folklore and Myth in the Mabinogion* (Cardiff: University of Wales Press, 1958).

Gruffydd, W.J., *Math Vab Mathonwy, An Inquiry into the Origins and Development of the Fourth Branch of the Mabinogi, with the Text and a Translation* (Cardiff: University of Wales Press Board, 1928).

Gruffydd, W.J., *Rhiannon: Inquiry into the First and Third Branches of the Mabinogion* (Cardiff: University of Wales Press Board,1953).

Hamp, Edward, "Mabinogi and Archaism", *Celtica 23,* (1999) pp. 96 – 110.

Harrison, Henry, *Surnames of the United Kingdom: A concise etymological dictionary, Volume 2* (London: Morland Press, Ltd., 1918).

Hemming, Jessica, "Reflections on Rhiannon and the Horse Episodes in 'Pwyll'", *Western Folklore, Vol. 57, No. 1* (Winter, 1998), 19 – 40

Hull, Eleanor, *The Cuchullin Saga in Irish Literature: being a collection of stories relating to the Hero Cuchullin,* (London: David Nutt, 1989).

Hutton, Ronald, "Medieval Welsh Literature and Pre-Christian Deities", *Cambrian Medieval Celtic Studies 61* (2011), 57 – 85

Jackson, Kenneth H., *The International Popular Tale and the Early Welsh tradition* (Cardiff: University of Wales Press, 1961)

Jones, Thomas Gwynn, *Welsh Folklore and Folk-Custom* (London: Methuen & Co., Ltd., 1930).

Koch, John T., editor, *Celtic Culture: An Historical Encyclopedia,* (Oxford, England: ABC-CLIO, 2006).

Linduff, Katheryn M., "Epona: A Celt Among the Romans", *Latomus, T. 38, Fasc. 4* (Octobre – Decembre, 1979), pp. 817 – 837.

Lyle, Emily B., "Dumezil's Three Functions and Indo-European Cosmic Structure", *History of Religions, Vol. 22, No. 1,* (Aug., 1982), 25 – 44.

Mac Cana, Proinsias, *The Mabinogi,* second edn., (Cardiff: University of Wales Press, 1992).

MacCulloch, J.A., *The Religion of the Ancient Celts,* (Edinburgh: T. & T. Clark, 1911).

McKenna, Catherine, "The Theme of Sovereignty in Pwyll," *Bulletin of the Board of Celtic Studies,* 29 (1980), 35 – 52.

Miles-Watson, Jonathan, *Welsh Mythology: A Neo-Structuralist Approach* (Amherst: Cambria Press, 2009).

Owen, Trefor M., *Welsh Folk Customs* (Llandysul: Gomer Press, 1985).

Rees, Alwyn and Rees Brinley, *Celtic Heritage: Ancient Tradition in Ireland and Wales* (London: Thames and Hudson, Ltd., 1961).

Reinach, Salomon, "Epona", *Revue Archéologique, Troisième Série, T. 26* (1895), 163 – 195

Ross, Anne, *Folklore of Wales* (Stroud: Tempus Publishing Ltd., 2001).

Ross, Anne, *Pagan Celtic Britain* (Chicago: Academy Chicago Publishers, 1996).

Stifter, David, *Old Celtic Languages,* (Sommersemester, 2008).

Sullivan, C. W., *The Mabinogi: A Book of Essays* (New York: Garland Publishing, Inc., 1996).

Thomas, Gwyn, *Tales from the Mabinogion* (Woodstock: The Overlook Press, 1984).

Thomas, Jenkin W., *The Welsh Fairy Book,* (New York: F. A. Stokes, 1908).

Thompson, Stith. *Motif-index of folk-literature: a classification of narrative elements in folktales, ballads, myths, fables, medieval romances, exempla, fabliaux, jest-books, and local legends.*

(Bloomington: Indiana University Press, 1955 – 1958). Available at http://www.ruthenia.ru/folklore/thompson/

Trevelyan, Marie, *Folk-Lore and Folk-Stories of Wales* (London: Elliot Stock, 1909).

Valente, Roberta Louise, "Merched Y Mabinogi: Women and the Thematic Structure of the Four Branches", (Unpublished Ph.D. Thesis, Cornell University, 1986).

Van der Linden, Renske, "The Laws of Hywel Dda in the Four Branches of the Mabinogi", (Unpublished M.A. Thesis, University of Utrecht, 2007).

Vermaat, Robert, "Modrun, granddaughter of Vortigern", retrieved from http://www.vortigernstudies.org.uk/artfam/modrun.htm.

Welsh, Andrew, "Doubling and Incest in the Mabinogi", *Speculum, Vol. 65, No. 2* (Apr., 1990), pp. 344 – 362.

Westropp, T.J., "Notes and Folklore from the Rennes Copy of the 'Dindsenchas'", *The Journal of the Royal Society of Antiquaries of Ireland Fifth Series, Vol. 9, No. 1* (Mar. 31, 1899), 21 – 27

Winward, Fiona, "The Women in the Four Branches", *Cambrian Medieval Studies 34* (1997), 77 – 106.

Wood, Juliette, "The Fairy Bride Legend in Wales", *Folklore, Vol. 103, No. 1* (1992), 56 – 72.

Wood, Juliette, "The Horse in Welsh Folklore: A Boundary Image in Custom and Narrative", *The Horse in Celtic Culture: Medieval Welsh Perspectives,* Davies, Sioned and Jones, Nerys Ann, eds., (Cardiff: University of Wales Press, 1997), 162 – 179

We think you will also enjoy...

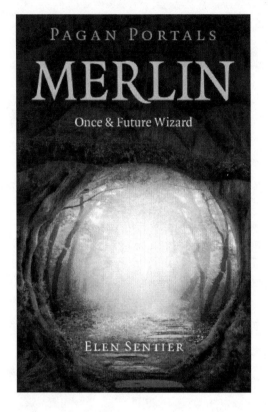

Merlin: Once and Future Wizard

Merlin in history, Merlin in mythology, Merlin through the
ages and his continuing relevance

*...a grand and imaginative work that introduces the reader to the
many faces of the mysterious Merlin.*
Morgan Daimler

978-1-78535-453-3 (paperback)
978-1-78535-454-0 (e-book)

Best Selling Pagan Portals & Shaman Pathways

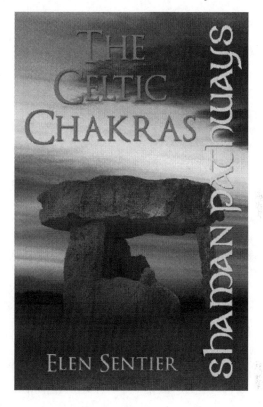

Celtic Chakras, Elen Sentier

Tread the British native shaman's path, explore the Goddess
hidden in the ancient stories; walk the Celtic chakra spiral
labyrinth.

*Rich with personal vision, the book is an interesting exploration of
wholeness*
Emma Restall Orr

978-1-78099-506-9 (paperback)
978-1-78099-507-6 (e-book)

Best Selling Pagan Portals & Shaman Pathways

Druid Shaman, Danu Forest

A practical guide to Celtic shamanism with exercises and techniques as well as traditional lore for exploring the Celtic Otherworld

A sound, practical introduction to a complex and wide-ranging subject
Philip Shallcrass

978-1-78099-615-8 (paperback)
978-1-78099-616-5 (e-book)

Kitchen Witchcraft, Rachel Patterson

Take a glimpse at the workings of a Kitchen Witch and
share in the crafts

*A wonderful little book which will get anyone started on Kitchen
Witchery. Informative, and easy to follow*
Janet Farrar & Gavin Bone

978-1-78099-843-5 (paperback)
978-1-78099-842-8 (e-book)

Best Selling Pagan Portals
& Shaman Pathways

Moon Magic, Rachel Patterson
An introduction to working with the phases of the Moon

*...a delightful treasury of lore and spiritual musings that should be
essential to any planetary magic-worker's reading list.*
David Salisbury

978-1-78279-281-9 (paperback)
978-1-78279-282-6 (e-book)

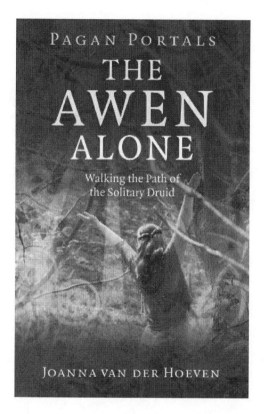

The Awen Alone, Joanna van der Hoeven
An introductory guide for the solitary Druid

*Joanna's voice carries the impact and knowledge of the ancestors,
combined with the wisdom of contemporary understanding.*
Cat Treadwell

978-1-78279-547-6 (paperback)
978-1-78279-546-9 (e-book)

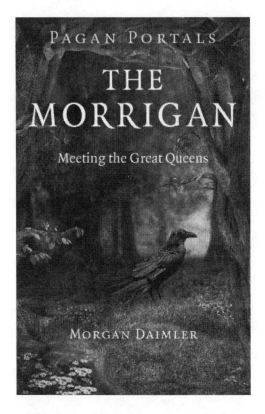

The Morrigan, Morgan Daimler

On shadowed wings and in raven's call, meet the ancient Irish
Goddess of war, battle, prophecy, death, sovereignty, and
magic

*...a well-researched and heartfelt guide to the Morrigan from a fellow
devotee and priestess*
Stephanie Woodfield

978-1-78279-833-0 (paperback)
978-1-78279-834-7 (e-book)

Moon Books

PAGANISM & SHAMANISM

What is Paganism? A religion, a spirituality, an alternative belief system, nature worship? You can find support for all these definitions (and many more) in dictionaries, encyclopaedias, and text books of religion, but subscribe to any one and the truth will evade you. Above all Paganism is a creative pursuit, an encounter with reality, an exploration of meaning and an expression of the soul. Druids, Heathens, Wiccans and others, all contribute their insights and literary riches to the Pagan tradition. Moon Books invites you to begin or to deepen your own encounter, right here, right now.

If you have enjoyed this book, why not tell other readers by posting a review on your preferred book site. Recent bestsellers from Moon Books are:

Journey to the Dark Goddess
How to Return to Your Soul
Jane Meredith
Discover the powerful secrets of the Dark Goddess and transform your depression, grief and pain into healing and integration.
Paperback: 978-1-84694-677-6 ebook: 978-1-78099-223-5

Shamanic Reiki
Expanded Ways of Working with Universal Life Force Energy
Llyn Roberts, Robert Levy
Shamanism and Reiki are each powerful ways of healing; together,
their power multiplies. *Shamanic Reiki* introduces techniques to
help healers and Reiki practitioners tap ancient healing wisdom.
Paperback: 978-1-84694-037-8 ebook: 978-1-84694-650-9

Pagan Portals – The Awen Alone
Walking the Path of the Solitary Druid
Joanna van der Hoeven
An introductory guide for the solitary Druid, *The Awen Alone* will
accompany you as you explore, and seek out your own place
within the natural world.
Paperback: 978-1-78279-547-6 ebook: 978-1-78279-546-9

A Kitchen Witch's World of Magical Herbs & Plants
Rachel Patterson
A journey into the magical world of herbs and plants, filled with
magical uses, folklore, history and practical magic. By popular
writer, blogger and kitchen witch, Tansy Firedragon.
Paperback: 978-1-78279-621-3 ebook: 978-1-78279-620-6

Medicine for the Soul
The Complete Book of Shamanic Healing
Ross Heaven
All you will ever need to know about shamanic healing and how to
become your own shaman…
Paperback: 978-1-78099-419-2 ebook: 978-1-78099-420-8

Shaman Pathways – The Druid Shaman
Exploring the Celtic Otherworld
Danu Forest
A practical guide to Celtic shamanism with exercises and
techniques as well as traditional lore for exploring the Celtic
Otherworld.
Paperback: 978-1-78099-615-8 ebook: 978-1-78099-616-5

Traditional Witchcraft for the Woods and Forests
A Witch's Guide to the Woodland with Guided Meditations and
Pathworking
Melusine Draco
A Witch's guide to walking alone in the woods, with guided
meditations and pathworking.
Paperback: 978-1-84694-803-9 ebook: 978-1-84694-804-6

Wild Earth, Wild Soul
A Manual for an Ecstatic Culture
Bill Pfeiffer
Imagine a nature-based culture so alive and so connected,
spreading like wildfire. This book is the first flame…
Paperback: 978-1-78099-187-0 ebook: 978-1-78099-188-7

Naming the Goddess
Trevor Greenfield
Naming the Goddess is written by over eighty adherents and
scholars of Goddess and Goddess Spirituality.
Paperback: 978-1-78279-476-9 ebook: 978-1-78279-475-2

Shapeshifting into Higher Consciousness
Heal and Transform Yourself and Our World with Ancient
Shamanic and Modern Methods
Llyn Roberts
Ancient and modern methods that you can use every day to
transform yourself and make a positive difference in the world.
Paperback: 978-1-84694-843-5 ebook: 978-1-84694-844-2

Readers of ebooks can buy or view any of these bestsellers by
clicking on the live link in the title. Most titles are published in
paperback and as an ebook. Paperbacks are available in traditional
bookshops. Both print and ebook formats are available online.

Find more titles and sign up to our readers' newsletter at
http://www.johnhuntpublishing.com/paganism
Follow us on Facebook at
https://www.facebook.com/MoonBooks
and Twitter at https://twitter.com/MoonBooksJHP